KNAP

BRIGHTON & HOVE

Look out for other great titles in
the Knapsack Guide Series

Knapsack Guide To London

Knapsack Guide To Disneyland Paris

Get your hands on them and start planning
some more exciting trips!

Where do you think we should do next?
Been somewhere interesting?

Let us know!
hello@knapsackguides.com

KNAPSACK GUIDE TO BRIGHTON & HOVE

essential guides for streetwise kids

Written and Researched
by
Michael and Helenor Rogers

Illustrations by Laura Broad

www.knapsackguides.com

Knapsack Guide to Brighton & Hove

Acknowledgements
Dedicated to everyone who helped us along the
way; with enormous thanks. Especially to our proof readers
(Joanne Gray, Elaine Spindlow and Andrew Osborne) and to
Glenys Morris and the kids from Westdene Library Book Club.

We proudly present the first ever Knapsack Guide.

First published in 2004.   phewwww!
Drafted, crafted and grafted by Helenor and
Michael Rogers. Groovy drawings and cartoons by
Laura Broad.

Lovingly Published by Knapsack Publishing Ltd.

Knapsack Publishing Ltd
PO Box 124
Hove
BN3 3UY

© Knapsack Publishing Ltd 2004.

Printed by the very nice people at Gutenberg Press Ltd.

Boring legal stuff...

All rights reserved. No part of this publication may
be reproduced, stored in a retrieval system, or
transmitted in any form or by any means, electronic,
photocopying, recording or otherwise - unless the
written permission of the publishers has been obtained
beforehand.

This book is sold subject to the condition that it shall not, by
way of trade or otherwise, be lent, resold, hired out or other
wise circulated without the publisher's prior consent.

ISBN: 0-9545212-0-X

Excuses...!!!
Whilst we have tried really hard to make this book as accurate
as possible, things have a habit of changing (especially in
Brighton!). We are sorry if we have got anything wrong. If you
find a mistake please let us know by contacting us at
hello@knapsackguides.com

CONTENTS

Introduction — 6

The Essentials — 8
- Planning and Preparation — 8
- Getting There/ Staying There — 10
- Useful Info — 16
- International Visitors — 20
- Special Needs — 23

The Facts — 25
- History — 25
- Geography — 28
- People of Brighton — 28
- The Gruesome Bits... — 29

Hanging Out — 33
- In Cool Places — 33
- With The Rich And Famous — 40
- Shopping — 42
- Sports — 50
- Cultural and Arty Stuff — 59
- Nosh — 62
- Back To Nature — 71
- Not Too Far Away — 76

The Ultimate — 80
- The Ultimate Day Out — 80
- The Ultimate Free Day Out — 83

Handy Stuff — 87
- Listings — 87
- Web Sites — 90

Index — 92

INTRODUCTION

Well you're really lucky to be going to Brighton & Hove! For years and years it has been a place of fun and frolics for people of all ages, you've just got to get down to the seaside. If you live there or nearby then even better, you can enjoy the delights it has to offer every weekend. It is a bit of a mad place full of all kinds of people doing all kinds of things, a real mix of the ultra cool and modern to historic and hysterical. You will love it!

About This Guide

There are so many guide books written for adults, but none for kids. So we thought it was about time you had your own guide. A guide book that tells you the things you want to know, not what people think you should know, in a way that is interesting, fun and a little bit cheeky!

We have tried to keep the layout simple and easy to use. It is split up into 5 main sections.

The Essentials - takes you through the basic things you need to think about to get the most out of where you are going and the best ways to get around when you are there.

The Facts - gives you the low down on all the key facts about Brighton & Hove and all the gruesome ones as well!

Hanging Out - gets down to the real nitty gritty and gives you all of the in-depth info on the best places to go, eat and be seen.

The Ultimate - takes all the info in this book and suggests some example ultimate days out. So if you are a lazy so and so and you really can't be bothered reading very much, that's the place to head for.

Handy Stuff - does exactly what it says and pulls together useful details such as addresses, telephone numbers and websites.

Ready to get started?

About Scout
You will find well travelled Scout throughout the book, giving you hints and tips and letting you in on insider secrets. He also knows loads of useful and useless facts and figures. You can find out more about Scout at www.knapsackguides.com

About www.knapsackguides.com
Don't forget to visit www.knapsackguides.com for all of the latest info on Brighton and Hove and links to all of the other websites mentioned in this book. There are loads of photos of the best sights and latest timings for the big events. You can also write to us so that other knapsackers can see what you have to say - your opinion counts! So get surfing.

Warning!
As much as we like to think we are perfect at Knapsack Publishing, the reality is we are not. We have checked and checked again to make sure all the information in here is correct, but prices change, people move and leave the country and shops, restaurants and attractions shut down. So if you find something that's not right please tell us about it. In fact we would love to hear from you about anything at all. You can contact us on hello@knapsackguides.com.

THE ESSENTIALS

Planning and Preparation

It might sound boring, but the best way to make sure you have the greatest time ever is to plan things in advance. Otherwise you might end up having to do the 'fun' things that the grown ups want to do every day. They really believe that going to an Art Exhibition to see an old painting by some mad French man

TOP TIPS TO GET YOUR OWN WAY

- Plan your trip in advance.
- Read about the places you want to go to, have some good reasons why you think this would be a good place to visit.
- Mention your ideas a while in advance, just casually, in conversation. Be persistent but not annoying.
- If you are going with other kids get them on your side. Show them where you want to go and get them to talk about how excited they are to be going there.
- Keep your room tidy, don't leave your shoes, bags and coat in the hall way and clean the goldfish. Don't give any excuses for not getting your way.
- Finally smile, be happy, and be enthusiastic about the trip. (Adults love that!!).

will thrill you to pieces, so unless this is your kind of thing you better come up with a different plan of action.

Find out roughly what you're supposed to be doing, even if it has already been agreed you might be able to wangle a bit of a detour if it's for a good cause. If nothing much has been arranged you can help everyone out by planning a day to remember. Much as we'd like to cover absolutely everywhere we only had room to cover what we think are the best places for kids, if you don't agree then let us know. We've grouped them by activity areas, although individual attractions can be found using the index at the back of the book.

Read all about it and then decide on what you fancy doing. Fill this in on a 'Day Planner' like the one below, you can print out copies of this from www.knapsackguides.com.

Day Planner

Start	End	What?	Why?	Cost

Things to Pack

Clothes are always useful as you don't want to be walking around naked, it can get a bit chilly by the sea! But seriously it's always best to be prepared so this is a good list of things to start with.

THINGS TO PACK

- A snazzy pair of trainers, good for walking around and great to show you know your bling.
- A camera for super snaps and embarrassing photos for blackmail later (see Money Making Scams).
- All weather protection gear (umbrella, sun cream, hat) be prepared for all eventualities.
- An emergency telephone number for distress situations (like your parent's mobile number).
- A good map. We've got an outline map in here, this is useful to give you a general idea of where places are but won't be any good for outlying missions. Get one from the Tourist Information Centres.
- Pen and a pad or your Knapsack Travelog, for notes or for detailing incriminating evidence.
- Some extra pocket money will be great - again check out "money making scams".
- A great guide book (oh you already have one!).

Getting There/ Staying There

There are quite a few ways to get to Brighton & Hove as it has been a popular tourist place for many, many years. You can fly in (if you are very rich), or come by train, bus or car. The grown ups might have already decided this, but we've included all the details in case you need to give them a bit of advice.

MONEY MAKING SCAMS

- Down the side of the sofa is always a good place to start.
- Start a swear box for the grown ups and then annoy them to get them really angry - watch it roll in...
- Get some super embarrassing stuff together (your sister's secret diary, baby photos of your big brother, your dad's hair dye, your mum's false boobs) anything they wouldn't want people to know about and charge them a small fee for their safe return.
- Working - the least enjoyable option but sometimes the last resort. Try washing cars, mowing lawns, going shopping, dog walking etc. Never do anything for free, your time is money man.

By Air

It is very unlikely that you will fly in to Brighton & Hove, but if you do you'll probably arrive at Gatwick Airport about 25 miles away. There is a railway station in the South Terminal where you can get a train directly to Brighton or Hove and they go around every 30 minutes. There is also a coach station and you could get a taxi; however the train is probably the quickest and easiest option. There is also a very small airport about 5 miles away at Shoreham, handy if you have your own private jet.

By Train

☎ National Rail Enquiries: 0845 7484950

Brighton & Hove each have a mainline station; you will probably arrive in Brighton (this one is nearest to all the fun and games). You can get direct trains from London Victoria (50 mins on the Brighton Express);

Kings Cross Thameslink and London Bridge stations. There are over 50 departures every day from London, a very regular service. You can also get direct trains to Brighton from Reading, Bristol and South Wales, Portsmouth and Southampton - and even from Scotland. Children get reduced fares so this really is the best option. The town and the sea are just a 10 minute walk from the station; it's all downhill on the way but it's all uphill on the way back so it takes a bit longer! It's really exciting when you arrive - first one to see the sea gets a prize!

By Car

Parking in Brighton & Hove is quite expensive (less to spend on having fun!) and the traffic is really bad so it is best not to drive into the city. It is better to park on the outskirts and either use the 'Park and Ride' scheme or take the train in to the city. The 'Park and

HOW TO DRIVE ADULT'S NUTS ON A CAR JOURNEY

- Don't go to the toilet before a long trip, ask to go after about ½ an hour driving.
- Offer to drive the car so they can get some sleep.
- Start a booming song of '999 Green Bottles Hanging On The Wall'.
- Ask every 30 seconds "are we there yet?"
- Wait until you are in the middle of nowhere and say you are starving.

Ride' car park is at the Withdean Stadium where Brighton & Hove Albion play football. This is easy to get to from the A23 or A27 and is quite cheap - it is free for up to 2 kids per adult; they have to pay £2 return each but this does include the parking. Many stations on the outskirts have parking and a regular, quick service into the city (National Rail Enquires can help with this).

But, if you really have to drive into the city the best places to park are either at Brighton Station (£10 per day) or along Madeira Drive next to the Palace Pier. Be warned, get there early.

By Coach

☎ Brighton & Hove Bus & Coach Company: 01273 886200
☎ National Express: 0870 5808080

National Express coaches arrive at Brighton from places all over the UK.
Both National Express and regional bus operators arrive at Pool Valley Bus Station on the Old Steine, just a few minutes walk from the city centre and the beach.

Getting Your Bearings

Brighton & Hove is quite an easy place to get your bearings as you can always use the sea as a reference point. Many of the streets are on a grid pattern (especially in Hove) making it easier to find places. The main sights and attractions are quite well signposted and tend to be around the Pavilion area or down by the Palace Pier and the sea.

The tricky bit comes around the Lanes. There are two areas of Lanes; the North Laine just down from Brighton Station and the Old Lanes just up from the sea going left from the Palace Pier. They are really cool, full of wacky shops. There are loads of stories that they were hang outs for smugglers, vagabonds and maybe still are for ghosts! (see the "The Facts" section).

WHAT IF I GET LOST?

- First thing, don't panic!! There are a number of things you can do. Look around and find out where you are, find out the street name and any other landmarks, post offices, pubs etc.
- If you have a good map look the address up and plan an escape route.
- If you see a Policeman, they will be more than happy to help.
- If you are by shops then do go in and ask the shopkeeper, they will usually help. Estate Agents sometimes give out free maps.
- Ask someone walking in the street, they might be able to help. Be careful if you do this there are some weirdo's about.

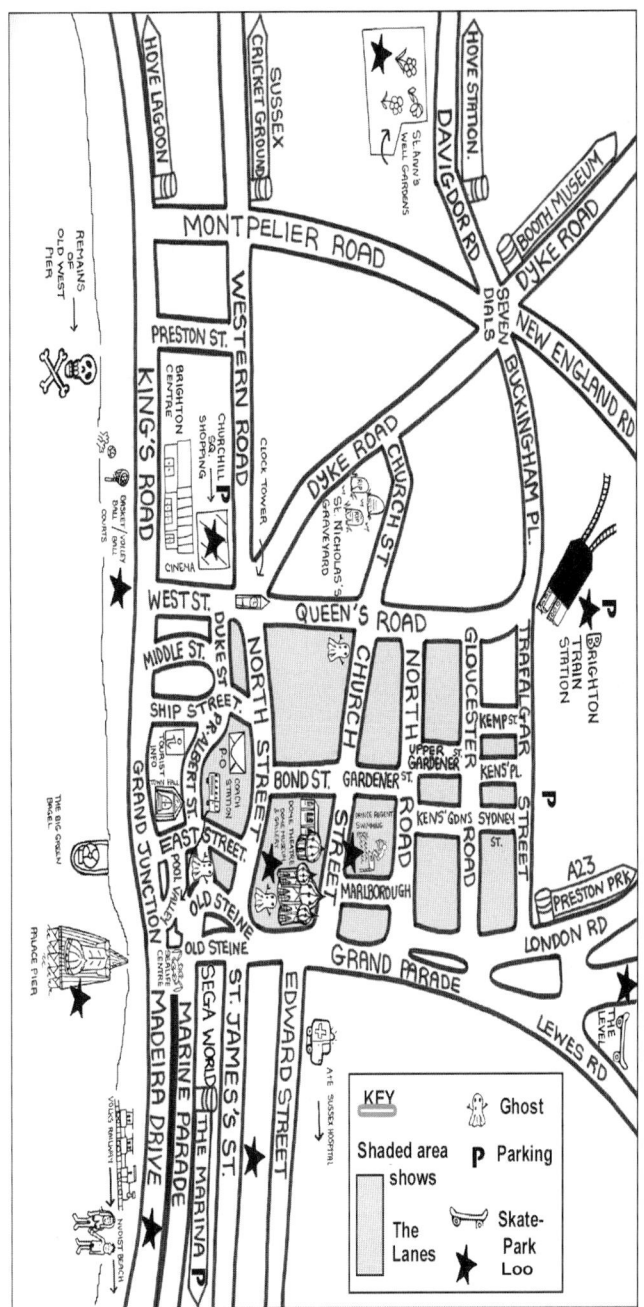

THE ESSENTIALS

You will almost certainly get lost in the Lanes, which is part of the fun. Just keep wandering around and enjoy the shops and cafes and if you really get lost ask for some help.

Getting Around

Walking
The most fun and probably the fastest way to get around Brighton & Hove is to walk. So many of the best bits are not far apart. You can easily walk to them and then you get to feel the Brighton vibe at the same time. This is really recommended, many of the sections of this book suggest walking around for most or part of the time. When you are out and about keep your eyes peeled and keep looking up as well as straight ahead, some of the most amazing sights will be above your head.

There are also a variety of guided walks through Brighton & Hove and around the beautiful countryside not far away. Walking might sound a bit crazy to you but hey, you've got legs, use them!

Local Buses
Brighton & Hove has an excellent local bus service; within the city centre and about 5 miles out in all directions you can make any journey for 60p for kids (under 14) and £1.20 for grown ups. Many of them are double-deckers (get the top front seats for the best view) and some of them even have a  special floor that moves down to let you get on easily. All of the buses are named after famous people who live or who have lived in the city, look out and see if you can spot anyone you recognise.

There are also all kinds of day / week passes that might be useful if you are planning on staying for a while or if you are going on quite a few trips. Some of the deals even let kids under 16 travel for free, now is that a bargain or what? There are also a few bus trips that link to some of the great walks in the countryside (see the "Hanging Out" section).

Taxis

Brighton & Hove Taxis are painted white and turquoise and most of them can be hailed from the street 24 hours a day. Some of them have to be booked in advance or picked up at recognised taxi ranks (see below). Fortunately the taxi numbers are incredibly easy to remember:

☎Taxi: 01273 20 20 20 or 01273 41 41 41

Key Taxi Ranks

Brighton Train Station	Brighton Bus Station
The Brighton Centre	Queen's Square near the Clock Tower
Hove Railway Station	Hove Town Hall

What do you call a girl with two toilets on her head? Lulu!!

I NEED A WEE!

- It happens to us all; you just can't enjoy yourself when you are desperate to go to the loo. The best options are:
- On the Pier - some of the nicest toilets in Brighton are to be found on the Palace Pier. They are quite far down, almost at the end, but worth the walk.
- Along the beach front - there are a few OK toilets along the front. The best ones are by the children's play area. There are also OK loos on the wide Esplanade in Hove and on Madeira Drive.
- Shopping Centres / Department Stores / Cinemas usually quite good, especially nice shops like Debenhams and the Churchill Square Centre.
- Fast food outlets - McDonalds, Burger King etc usually have OK toilets, but sometimes they get a bit cross if you don't buy the food!
- Train Station - not usually terribly pleasant and a rip off at 20p, the gents are especially bad in Brighton.
- In the public sports centres / swimming pools.
- Brighton Museum & Art Gallery and Hove Museum have nice clean, free loos.
- In the big parks / Pavilion Gardens.

THE ESSENTIALS

Places to Stay

There are lots of places to stay over in Brighton & Hove. From camp sites to bed and breakfasts to posh hotels, there is quite a lot of choice. Good value, family friendly hotels include the Quality Inn, the Premier Lodge and the Travelodge; a beautiful but more expensive family friendly hotel is the Alias Hotel Seattle in the Marina. Other hotels and B&B's often do good deals, especially outside of the peak season and at the last minute.

☎ Quality Inn: 020 8298 7272
☎ Premier Lodge: 0870 9906340
☎ Travelodge: 0870 0850950
☎ Alias Hotel Seattle: 01273 679799

Useful Info

The Weather

How do you know when it's been raining cats and dogs? There are loads of poodles everywhere!

If you talk to anyone in the UK it is very likely that the subject of the weather will come up. Everyone talks about the weather whether it is hot or cold, dry or rainy; it's a good conversation maker. Generally this is because the weather is never that great. Brighton & Hove weather is much the same as the rest of the UK. Each season has its own charm with Spring and Autumn being good times to visit without the summer crowds.

The table (top right) shows the weather you can expect in Brighton & Hove, but be prepared, it's not always what it's supposed to be. You can have really bright sunny days in February and pouring wind and rain in August, one of the joys of the British climate.

The hills of the South Downs act as a barrier to the city, often protecting it from the bad weather, giving the town a special 'micro-climate'. So even if the weather doesn't look great on your way here don't despair, it may brighten up as you get closer.

Weather Stats

	J	F	M	A	M	J	J	A	S	O	N	D
Avg. Max (°C)	7	7	9	12	16	19	22	21	18	15	10	7
Avg. Min (°C)	0	0	1	3	6	9	11	11	8	6	3	1
Mean (°C)	3	4	6	8	11	14	17	16	14	11	7	4
Rainfall (mm)	79	51	61	53	56	56	46	56	69	74	76	79

The 'Mean' doesn't mean nasty or stingy - it is the average temperature for that month. So the average temperature you can expect to find in Brighton and Hove in July is 17°C, although on average it could get as hot as 22°C or as cold as 11°C.

What's On And When

Whenever you come to Brighton & Hove there will be lots to do, but there are some extra special events that happen around the same time every year. Please check www.knapsackguides.com for precise dates. The best ones are the five smile events below:

Month	Events	Rating
January	New Years Eve Celebrations	☺☺
February	Brighton Half Marathon Race	☺
March	Not a lot happens - great waves when the big winds start blowing!	☺
April	British Juggling Convention - University of Sussex	☺☺
May	Brighton Festival throughout the month Royal Escape Race - Brighton to France boat race commemorating the journey of King Charles II	☺☺☺☺ ☺☺
June	London To Brighton Bike Race Party In The Park - Preston Park	☺☺☺ ☺☺☺☺☺
July	Kite Festival - Stanmer Park	☺☺☺☺
August	Gay Pride Parade - City and Preston Park	☺☺☺
September	Basketball season starts (Brighton Bears)	☺☺☺☺☺
October	Political Party Conferences (boring!!) Halloween Parties & Fireworks on the Pier	No Smiles!! ☺☺☺
November	Bonfire Night (Lewes Bonfire Night Celebration is amazing)	☺☺☺☺ ☺☺
December	Burning Of The Clocks Parade (on the shortest day around the 22nd)	☺☺☺☺

PUBLIC HOLIDAYS

New Years Day:	January 1
Good Friday:	Late March / Early April
Easter Monday:	After Good Friday, Late March / Early April
May Day:	First Monday in May
Whitsun Holiday:	Last Monday in May
August Bank Holiday:	Last Monday in August
Christmas Day:	25th December
Boxing Day:	26th December

If either of the Christmas or New Year holidays falls on Saturday or Sunday the following weekday becomes a public holiday

Shop Opening Hours

Nowadays shops in Brighton & Hove tend to be open 7 days a week, although some shops are only open for 6 hours on a Sunday. You might think shopkeepers in Brighton are really lazy on Sundays as many of the shops don't open until after 11am, but this is because many people have been out the night before so there aren't many shoppers around until lunchtime. This is especially true around the famous shopping Lanes. Shops open about 9am ish, closing around 5.30pm. Thursday night is late night opening.

Lurgies

The UK is very safe when it comes to health and Brighton & Hove is no exception. There are very few diseases around and the animals usually are not deadly, there is really nothing to worry about. The local hospitals and doctors will accept non-local and international visitors if you have a problem. Pharmacies are a good place to go for a quick response. There are pharmacies in all of the main shopping streets, 'Boots', 'Lloyds' and 'Superdrug' are the biggest chains. Grown ups can buy medicines in these places and there are trained Pharmacists who can give help and advice.

THE ESSENTIALS

Hopefully you won't need to know this bit; but it's here just in case. If you have an accident and need an emergency repair job done you can be taken to the A&E (Accident and Emergency) department at the Royal Sussex County Hospital. To get there you need to follow the coast road (A259) towards the Marina in the direction of Newhaven. The A&E hospital is sign-posted before you reach the Marina on the left hand side.

✉ Accident And Emergency Department
Royal Sussex County Hospital
Eastern Road
Brighton

☎ 01273 696955

Alternatively if it's just advice that is needed get a grown up to call NHS Direct on 08-45-46- 47. This line is open 24 hours every day.

BODY FACTS

- Placed end to end, all your body's blood vessels would measure about 62,000 miles.
- You have about 100,000 hairs on your head.
- You blink your eyes about 20,000 times a day.
- When you sneeze, air rushes through your nose at a rate of 100 mph - watch out for supersonic snot!!
- An eyelash lives for 150 days before it falls out.
- Most people shed 20 kilos of skin in a lifetime - yuck!
- You use 14 muscles to smile and 43 to frown.

Why did the skull go to the disco on his own? He had nobody to go with!!

In case of a real medical emergency or serious accident or if you need the Police, Fire Brigade or Coast Guard you should telephone 999 from any telephone and clearly ask for help, telling the person on the end of the line your name, where you are and details about the problem. It is very important that you only do this in an emergency, if you cause a false alarm you might stop the emergency services going to a real accident and someone else might die. You will get into big trouble so be warned!

COOL CURES

It's always handy to have a few miracle cures up your sleeve....

Hiccups: either hold your breath and count slowly to 30 (best with your eyes shut) or drink out of a glass of water from the back of the glass by drinking it upside down (ask a grown-up to show you-they will get really wet!)

Spots: lightly cover offending area with (red) stripy toothpaste

Nausea: steadily drink a glass of flat coke

Stomach ache: drink lots of ginger beer and burp a lot, or else drink freshly boiled water that has cooled down and lie down with a hot water bottle

Cure all - sleep lots and lots and / or eat chocolate ice cream.

WEIRD OLD CURES

Cures from the old days (don't try these at home unless you are completely bonkers!)

For whooping cough get some brown mice, bake them gently in the oven and eat them with raw onions - yuck!

For bed wetting burn a live mouse until it is turned to ash, sprinkle on top of jam and eat a spoonful before going to bed.

If you get jaundice (a liver disease where your skin turns yellow), swallow a live spider wrapped in butter.

Stop a bleeding cut or gash by wrapping it in a spider's web.

Rub warts with a piece of bloody, raw meat and then flush the meat down the loo.

International Visitors
(though interesting for everyone else too ...)

Time to.....
Have you seen the time written as say 08:00 GMT? GMT means Greenwich Mean Time, the time in Greenwich in East London (and the rest of the UK), and the standard time for the whole world. The time

in other countries is written compared to the time in Greenwich, for example Paris is GMT +1 hour and New York is GMT -5 hours so 08:00 in Brighton & Hove is 09:00 in Paris and 02:00 in New York. Greenwich is really where time started as we know it today!

Wonga... Wad... Dosh...

These are all words for money (also called currency). The UK's currency is pounds sterling (£). Each pound is made up of 100 pence (p).

If you want to know what the money in your country is worth in pounds sterling you need to check the exchange rate. This shows how much £1 is equal to in your currency. You can find out the latest exchange rates through the link on www.knapsackguides.com. Type in how much money you have saved for your trip and the currency you have saved it in and it will tell you how much you have in UK pounds.

Phrasebook

Of course the language used in Brighton & Hove is English. Duh! However back in the days gone by the locals used some great words.

Tell your mate a slummocky dinlow is a trendy dude - they won't know any better!

OLD SUSSEX WORDS

Spruser = conman
Dinlow = idiot
Kiddie = work mate / colleague
Slummocky = untidy
Slouchpudde = someone who staggers when walking.
Scurrywinkle = dart around / move quickly
Miriander = slow / stupid person
Catchmeddler = nosey person
Spirimawgus = ghost

Keeping in Touch

Telephone

Most people in the UK now have mobile telephones so there are less public phone boxes than there used to be. However there are still some around, especially in the centre of Brighton & Hove. You might even see some of the old traditional red boxes if you keep your eyes peeled. Most of these take coins and also credit or phone cards that you can buy from newsagents.

The telephone code for all numbers in Brighton & Hove is 01273. If you are calling a number from outside the UK you should dial the code to make an international call (often 00), then 44 for the UK and then miss the first zero starting the Brighton & Hove number with 1273 adding the rest of the numbers.

Snail Mail

 You can post letters at post offices or in post boxes making sure you have the correct stamp. Post boxes are also called pillar-boxes and are bright red.

Post Offices

There are four main post offices in the city centre, see Handy Stuff for locations.

POSTING CARD & LETTERS

- First Class post costs from 28p and should reach destination next day (yeah right!)
- Second Class post costs from 20p and should take 2-4 days.
- For International cards and letters you need a special stamp and an airmail sticker. The cost will depend on the weight and the destination. Europe is cheaper than the rest of the world.

E-mail

It is always good to set up an e-mail account that you can access from anywhere. There are instructions on www.knapsackguides.com showing you how to do this. Popular choices are 'hotmail' or 'yahoo'. There are many Internet cafés in Brighton & Hove where you can send e-mail or access www.knapsackguides.com to find out the latest news about what is on in Brighton & Hove.

Using the Internet
Remember to be careful when you are using the internet, especially when you are in chat rooms. NEVER give your name and address and NEVER meet anyone you make friends with unless you have the full approval of your parents and/or guardian. This might sound dull but it is really important, just don't put yourself at risk.

Special Needs
Brighton and Hove is one of the first cities in Britain to be included in the DisabledGo website. DisabledGo's mission is to open places up to hearing impaired, mobility impaired and vision impaired people and carers by providing detailed access information for all kinds of places from art galleries to swimming pools and theatres to zoos. The internet site is great containing all kinds of useful information.

Whilst Brighton & Hove has facilities for people of all abilities the historic nature of some of the sights makes it difficult for disabled visitors, especially for those that need wheelchair access. The cobbled streets in the Old Lanes, the stairs and uneven floors

TOP 5 PLACES FOR KIDS WITH SPECIAL NEEDS
- The Palace Pier
- The Seafront (not the pebbly beach!)
- The Brighton Bears Basketball Match (you get great seats!!)
- Bowlplex in Brighton Marina
- Churchill Square Shopping Centre

in the historic buildings and the pebbles on the beach are just not wheelchair friendly!

But do not despair! The Pier is great, long and flat so very easy to navigate. The Esplanade in Hove is fab for wheelchair racing; you could even try wheelchair kiting! You can access shops and galleries on the lower Esplanade in Brighton using the numerous

THE ESSENTIALS

ramps, whilst the Churchill Square Shopping Centre has wheelchair access and plenty of space even though it does get busy. The Brighton Museum & Art Gallery has wheelchair access but makes little provision for visually impaired visitors. The Brighton Dome, Corn Exchange and the Royal Pavilion also have wheelchair access. If you are visually impaired then you might like the scented gardens in St Ann's Well Gardens in Hove, a paradise for fragrant herbs and lightly perfumed flowers.

The Tourist Information Centre is fully accessible to the disabled and packs are available giving useful information on access to tourist attractions, public transport, sports facilities, pubs and restaurants, holiday accommodation, the seafront, shopping, public and essential services and other facilities.

For those with hearing difficulties, communication via Minicom is possible on (01273) 292595. Events and information lists are translated into braille and distributed to Brighton and Hove libraries. You can also get guides for Disabled Visitors to Brighton and Hove from Brighton and Hove Council Disability Advice Centre on 01273 203 016.

THE FACTS

History
Where it all began...
The history of Brighton & Hove spans nearly 2000 years, beginning shortly after the Romans invaded Britain in AD 43. Remains of a Roman Villa and Roman coins have been found in the town. The Doomsday Book (the big register of all the towns compiled in 1086) called it Bristelmestune and said that the town of 400 people had to pay taxes to the huge sum of 4000 herrings. Over the years the name was changed to Brightelmstone and then to Brighton and now to Brighton and Hove.

When you wander around the web of narrow streets and passageways of the Old Lanes you will be following the footsteps of the rugged ancient smugglers who use to hang out in the dark shadows doing their dodgy deals. Despite the threats from shady smugglers and niggles from nasty

What do you get if you cross a fish and a deaf person? A herring aid!

DID YOU KNOW?

Guess what a twitten is... It isn't an old fashioned name for an idiot or for an owl; it is actually an old Sussex word for a narrow path usually between two walls or hedges and often leading from one street to another. There are lots of twittens in the Lanes.

Whilst we are at it...do you know where 'Laine' comes from? No, it isn't a spelling mistake; there should be an 'i' in it. Laine comes from the Anglo-Saxon word that means lease. In the 1800's this part of Brighton was farming land that was divided into small areas leased to local farmers, these leased areas were called 'Laines'. Later in the 1800's the area was developed with housing, workshops and little businesses, the remains of which you can see today.

What about Catcreeps? It might sound like a made up name, but they are actually the flights of steps connecting two streets on different levels on a hill. Again you can find quite a few around Brighton, more around the North Laine and the Station.

French invaders who set fire to the place a couple of times, the little village grew.

Royal Visitors

The first royal visitor was Charles II. He was in a bit of trouble after his Cavaliers were beaten by the Roundheads at the Battle of Worcester in 1651. He escaped to Brighton disguised as a servant. He stayed at the Georges Inn in West Street (later renamed the Kings Head) and then sailed away in a boat to France. There is an annual Brighton to France boat race called the 'Royal Escape Race' held in his honour every May.

Chilly Dipping!

Brighton really came into its own in the 1750's. The sleepy little fishing village began to prosper after Dr Richard Russell from nearby Lewes publicised his amazing sea water cure that could solve everything from boils to bunions. Brighton became the place to go for the rich and famous Londoners.

DID YOU KNOW?

Boils are infections made by the rather nasty bacteria Staphylococcus aureus. Boils are called furuncles by Doctors and when several furuncles join together they are called a carbuncle!

Lots of local people became involved in the therapy, getting jobs helping the sick or the vain get into the water. They were called 'dippers' and basically shoved people into the water if they were being a bit pathetic. You might need a dipper yourself; the sea is like a liquid freezer even in the middle of summer.

The Prince Regent

Brighton was a real favourite of the Prince Regent, Prince George (who became George IV). He liked it so much he decided to build himself a little pad and then moved down. He was a bit of a flamboyant, fun loving chap and got a little carried away as you can see from the design of the Royal Pavilion; it's a bit different to Buckingham Palace or Windsor Castle don't you think? Believe it or not, it started as a simple farmhouse that had an extension added in 1787; before long it had all kinds of turrets and domes attached to the outside and the Chinese interior installed. It was kind of like 'Changing Rooms' of the 18th Century, the Prince's advisors must have been relations of Lawrence Llewellyn-Bowen!

Once the Prince Regent made Brighton his home and the railway was built, it became even more popular for the trendy London types who came on down in their masses. This allowed lots of new businesses to spring up and the tourist trade really began.

Around 1810 the town name changed to Brighton and the coat of arms was granted in 1897. This has two black dolphins in the middle surrounded by six little golden birds called martlets, finished off with a fetching blue border.

DID YOU KNOW?

Martha Gunn was a famous dipper, you can find out more about her at the Brighton Museum and also see her grave in St Nicholas's churchyard. She was good mates with the Prince Regent and often went down to the Pavilion for parties.

One night she was hanging about gossiping in the kitchen before dinner. The crafty Prince Regent noticed her sneakily slip a block of butter into her big flouncy skirt. Feeling a little mischievous he walked across to the roaring fire and called Martha over for a friendly chat. As they talked away the butter slowly melted in Martha's pocket trickling gently down her legs. Martha was well and truly caught, but the Prince let her off with a quick telling off!

Brighton Grows

As the town expanded, more housing was needed; especially for the rich Londoners. Brunswick Town was built on the outskirts of Hove, which then grew rapidly with its lovely long avenues and pretty squares.

When George IV died in 1830 his brother William IV used the Royal Pavilion as his seaside home in the seven years he was king. However his successor, their niece Queen Victoria, wasn't quite so keen. She really didn't like the Royal Pavilion as it didn't offer much privacy. She preferred to stay with friends in a grand house in Hove. In 1850 she sold the Pavilion to the Brighton Corporation for a bargain of £50,000.

Geography

Brighton & Hove is 51 miles south of London, in the county of East Sussex. With 7 miles of coastline in the city itself and 47 miles of coast across the county you are never far from the sea. The rolling South Downs protect the city from the weather and are a fantastic place for country walks or exciting sports like kiting and mountain biking.

> **DID YOU KNOW?**
> Some guy at one of the local universities estimates that there are approximately 100 billion pebbles on Brighton & Hove beach. If you counted one pebble every second it would take you 2,500 years to add them all up!

The beaches along the Sussex coast are mainly pebbled, although there is a little sand in Littlehampton and lots of sand in the east of the county around Rye. The hills and cliffs are generally made of chalk, you can tell this by the white cliffs next to the marina and you can even find pieces of chalk at the bottom of the cliffs amongst the pebbles in Saltdean.

People of Brighton

Nearly 250,000 people live in Brighton & Hove. This is a lot more than the 400 who lived here in 1086! There are almost 40,000 kids under the age of 15, equally split between boys and girls. Some of the people who live in Brighton & Hove come from all over the world, about 2,500 people come from outside the UK. Many people also come to Brighton & Hove to study, there are around 10,000 students. Finally there are the tourists, it is even more unbelievable that 8 million people come to visit Brighton & Hove every year. Brighton Palace Pier is the 4th most visited attraction in the country and the North Laine was voted the second 'Coolest Place in Britain' - must be worth a visit!

The Gruesome Bits...

Believe it or not, Brighton has been called the murder capital of Britain. Is that scary or what? Not to worry because nowadays it's a lot safer.

The trendy Lanes used to be well dodgy, they were the poorest and shabbiest areas of Brighton and many a murder would take place, often involving ladies of the night. At the start of the 20th century in the roaring 1920's, when Brighton was teeming with gangsters, murders were abound.

The Trunk Murders

A famous case was the 'trunk murders', where two suitcases were found containing gruesome dead bodies just a couple of weeks apart. To start with everyone assumed the cases must be linked - but in fact they were not. There were 2 murderers on the loose with completely different motives but very similar ways of disposing of their victims.

Brighton is also famous for something else quite horrid; it is the only place in Britain where a Chief Constable was murdered in his own police station. Now you would think a police station would be a pretty safe place, but obviously not for this poor man!

> What do you call a policeman with his fingers in his ears?
> Anything you like, he can't hear you!

Ghosts and Ghouls

As you can imagine along with murders tend to come ghosts; and Brighton and the surrounding district is home to quite a few of these too! In fact, Brighton is one of the most haunted places in England and the Old Lanes is the most haunted part of town. It sends a shiver down your spine doesn't it?

Nun Too Nice!

Amongst the famous ghosts is the nun who was bricked up alive for committing a terrible sin; she snogged a soldier and then ran away with him - a very bad thing for a nun to do! Religious people didn't like to spill blood, so they just build a tiny little box, put the nun in it and left her to starve to death. How nice. The poor soldier also met a bitter end; he was executed for leaving the army without permission. The nun has been seen around Meeting House Lane. Look out for her.

> What do you get if you cross a ghost and a pair of glasses?
> Spook-tacles!!

Town Hall Spooks

Apparently three ghosts haunt the Town Hall in the Old Lanes; a naughty monk, the Chief Constable (the one murdered in his own police station) and the Matron of the Workhouse that was once nearby.

Don't Lose Your Head

If you go to the Racecourse then look out for the headless horseman galloping across the Downs. He was the unfortunate victim of a false start at one of the early race meetings in the 18th Century. His horse got a bit over excited and surged forward just as the starting line snapped up; the line slid through the poor jockey's neck like a knife through cheese, leaving his skull rolling around the other horses hooves whilst his horse and the rest of his body galloped towards the finish line.

> What sort of horses do ghosts ride?
> Night mares!

The Manor House

Preston Manor (on the A23 on the road into Brighton) has been the site of a number of ghostly sightings;

generally of a white lady. Ghosts have been seen lots of times from the 16th century right up to 1993; during the late 19th century she was appearing about once every 6 weeks. The white lady can speak; an army colonel asked her who she was, she replied that she was a nun that had been chucked out of the church. When she died she was not allowed to be buried in holy ground or given a proper religious ceremony so she just couldn't rest in peace and took to haunting instead.

More recently in 1993, a security officer at Preston Manor saw the ghost of a lady dressed in black, walking across a landing in the house. She disappeared into a room, when he followed her she had gone. Just before her appearance he noticed the room suddenly went very cold and his head began to prickle; so if you notice these tell tale signs watch out!

TOP 5 PLACES TO SPOT GHOSTS
- The Old Lanes
- The Royal Pavilion
- The Town Hall
- Preston Manor
- Whitehawk Down (near the Racecourse)

Dome Lady
Another white lady has been seen in the Brighton Dome, it is thought she is the ghost of King George IV's boring wife Maria Fitzherbert. She has been seen in various places around what is now the theatre; she might even be sitting next to you especially if you are in the balcony.

Dipper Ghost
The ghost of Martha Gunn, the famous dipper, was seen in the banqueting room of the Royal Pavilion in the 1930's. A caterer was just checking everything was in order before a big banquet and was surprised to see someone else doing the same. An old, round lady wearing a long, heavy skirt, shawl and a big bon-

THE FACTS

net was wandering around and then flew right through the closed doors. Of course, when he rushed out to follow her the corridor was empty. He was keen to try to find out who the mystery woman might be; whilst looking through some old photographs he saw Martha Gunn and recognised her as the ghost.

Out and About

It's not just the city itself that is haunted; the surrounding Sussex countryside has lots of tales of ghosts and ghouls. Amongst the favourites are the 'wish hounds' or 'witch hounds'; the ghosts of a pack of hunting dogs that you can hear up at Ditchling Beacon. You can hear the cries of the hounds as well as the clattering of the horse's hooves and the hooting of the huntsmen's horn. There haven't been any sightings since the 1930's so you should be safe - or maybe you will be the latest person to witness this vision. Yikes!

And you thought Brighton & Hove was just a cool seaside city. The city's past is far more sinister than that!

HANGING OUT

Hanging Out - In Cool Places

The Seafront

One of the main reasons to go to Brighton & Hove is to go to see the sea. This was why tourists came here in the first place and is still why thousands make their way down to the coast on those rare beautiful days we get once a year in July!

The seafront is impressive. It is not the cheap, tacky place with hundreds of deckchairs, teenagers and men with hankies on their heads like some seaside towns. In fact, it is often called 'London by the sea', because of the cool people, great shops and buzzing atmosphere. Now you might moan because of the pebbles - but don't they are in fact very comfortable and very practical. Just put a towel down and wriggle about a bit - an instant back massage. Unlike at sandy beaches you don't end up with crunchy sandwiches and you do get a game of 'skimming the stones' thrown in for free. There, that's told you!

> **TOP 5 THINGS TO DO ON THE SEAFRONT**
> - People Watch / Chill / Sunbathe (with Factor 15 on of course)
> - Go to the Palace Pier
> - Shop
> - Skateboard / Rollerblade
> - Listen to the Buskers

> Why did the pebble blush?
> Because the sea weed!

On the Brighton side the seafront 'Esplanade' is set down from the road, so it is traffic-free and you are more or less walking on the beach but without the inconvenience of the pebbles. The road above is supported by arches at sea level, which have been converted into shops (mainly local crafts, beach clothing,

Hanging out

and souvenirs), and bars and restaurants, as well as some handy toilets!

The nearer you get to Palace Pier, the busier it gets, but even on a sunny Bank Holiday you can find some space if you take a walk westwards towards Hove. Be careful if you walk eastwards towards the Marina, behind that big hump of stones half way down is the Nudist Beach, with not the prettiest sights to be seen; probably best avoided! However just to the side of the Pier is Segaworld so if you've got a bit of time and a bit of cash you know where to spend it.

There are also many sporting facilities down the front such as a beach volleyball court, a basketball court, a skateboard area and a gravel pitch for playing boules. Specific information about these can be found out from the local authority's seafront offices just down from the beach volley court. The place feels very cosmopolitan, on a nice sunny day you can't beat it.

The Sea

The Sea itself is great, but watch out it is really, really cold. Even on the warmest, muggiest day the water is still absolutely freezing, quite refreshing, but cold. You see mad people going for a dip all through the year; there is an organisation of complete nutters who aim to take to the waters every day whatever the weather. Must be bonkers.

Unfortunately neither Brighton nor Hove is a Blue Flag beach, so the cleanliness can't be guaranteed. If this kind of things worries you then check out www.knapsackguides.com for a link to 'Surfers against Sewage' where you can find out the latest about the state of the waves

The Palace Pier

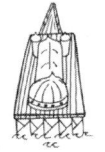

The Palace Pier, the place to have fun! Whether it is rainy or the sun is shining the Pier is the place you must go. So, maybe it is a bit tacky with the win a rubbish cuddly toy stalls, but it does have some good rides and some great games in the arcade. There are also some souvenir shops and places where you can have your signature analysed and your palm read.

All along the Pier there are little sign posts detailing its history. There are also a few funny picture stops where you can have your photo taken with you dressed up as a bride or in 1920's swim gear. One thing to note is the height restrictions for littlies on some of the more exciting rides.

There are two big arcades with loads and loads of games. Most cost about £1 per game so again you might have to save up.

If you are hungry on the Pier you can get good old fish and chips and then lots of stuff that is bad for you but tastes scrumptious like doughnuts, candy floss and ice cream. Just don't stuff your face before you go on the rides... you wouldn't want the food to repeat on you now would

> **PALACE PIER**
>
> 3,000 light bulbs illuminated the Palace Pier when it opened in 1899. Over a hundred years later it is illuminated by 13,000 light bulbs.

> **FREE ARCADE GAMES**
>
> Grown ups are usually really competitive - especially men. Tell them you will beat them at whatever game you fancy playing. Keep going on about how much more you will get than them. If they disagree then say 'Prove it' - they will then stump up the cash for you and them to have a go. Good one eh?

you? Imagine those poor people underneath you - eughhhhh!

Have a good look around and then chill out in the free deckchairs, this is a great place to watch the sun set on a beautiful day (if you ignore the horrid dock at Shoreham!).

The West Pier

The poor West Pier. It's a tragedy, OK maybe that's an exaggeration, but it is very sad to see what has happened to it. It has been closed since 1975 and will apparently be renovated and opened up again sometime - before it collapses entirely and falls into the sea. Spare a thought for the millions of little starlings that used to live inside that are now homeless - shame (oh well!).

The Victorian Penny Arcade

There is an old but interesting penny arcade down towards the Palace Pier where you can have a go on machines your great granny might have played. You pay 50p and you get 5 Victorian pennies to use on all the old machines. They are really funny and some are a bit naughty, so watch out.

If you have a little sister get her to try the 'Electric Tickler', it'll give her a little (but not unpleasant) electric shock, worth a laugh! I wouldn't trust the fortune telling machines, they only tell you good things.

The Big Green Doughnut

This is the massive green thing on the stone jetty not far from the Palace Pier. There is a bit of confusion about where this came from, some claim the Mayor of

Naples sent it as a gift after Brighton gave his town a large bronze herring. Or maybe it is just a groovy sculpture by local artist Hamish Black. The official name for it is 'Afloat', but you can call it the 'Seasick Doughnut'. You either like it or loathe it, some locals have tried to damage it to no avail and unlike the Piers even the weather won't hurt it. The holes in it are part of the design.

Volks Railway

The miniature Volks Railway runs along the seafront, down Madeira Drive, from the east of the Palace Pier all the way to the Marina. Thankfully it is low down so you don't get an eyeful when you pass the Nudist Beach. This railway has run along this stretch since 1883 using the same track and carriages. When the grown ups squeeze into the seats, you can remind them of how much bigger they have got compared to the small people in the old days.

If you go on the railway then either pop down to the Marina (see the boats, play ten pin bowling, shop, go to the cinema) or take the train back. There isn't much else to do along this glorified car park except for a tiny crazy golf course, the rest has been knocked down. Don't worry, you haven't missed much.

Madeira Drive

Sometimes there are some spectacles to be seen down this way - look out for the annual Bus Fiesta where you can watch hundreds of the bald, round, little coach owners proudly displaying their shiny vehicles and having tricky parking competitions. This is not made up, honest. There are also cooler events like the Beach Football competition, the Brighton ½ marathon, Mini car rallies, the end of the London to Brighton cycle race and the parades around Gay Pride and the Brighton & Hove Festival.

The Royal Pavilion

- Pavilion Buildings, Brighton
- Tel: 01273 290900
- Open daily June to September 10am-6pm, October to May 10am-5pm. Closed 25 & 26 December.
- £ Kids £3.40, Adults £5.80, OAPs £4, Family £15 (2 adults, 4 kids) / £9.20 (1 adult, 4 kids)

The most famous and one of the coolest buildings ever, has got to be the Royal Pavilion. It looks like a mini Taj Mahal and is a must visit place, even if you don't go inside.

The magnificent, crazy palace of the Prince Regent is right in the middle of the town centre, with lovely gardens all around. You can have a guided tour of the palace's mad but slightly musty interior or just wander around on your own. The best places are the mega kitchen with plenty of polished pots and pans and Queen Victoria's bedroom with her tiny wooden toilet next door - just imagine her perched on it! She cer-

> **DID YOU KNOW?**
> There are supposedly hidden underground passageways between the Royal Pavilion and the house where the Prince Regent's secret girlfriend lived in Old Steine (now the YMCA).

tainly would not be amused!! The enormous dining room table is amazing; it would be a great place to have your birthday party. There are special activities in the school holidays doing quite unusual things like stained glass workshops and Indian dance classes.

St Nicholas's Graveyard

Alright, this might be a bit morbid, but graveyards are quite interesting don't you think? Does the hair on the back of your neck stand up when you imagine the ghosts slipping out from under those huge stone coffins in the dark of the night? Imagine the bones deep under your feet, bones that have been there for hundreds of years.... spooky or what? St Nicholas's graveyard is especially intriguing as some of the graves are really old and some of the characters buried are very interesting. This is where the infamous Martha Gunn is buried, her grave is just to the right of the church as you look towards the sea. Next to that is the grave of the amazing lady, Pheobe Hessel.

DID YOU KNOW?

Pheobe Hessel was born in Stepney, London, in 1713 and had an amazing life, living to 108 - unheard of in those days. She fell in love with a private in the army when she was just 15 and didn't want to leave him. So she disguised herself as a man, enlisted in the 5th Regiment and followed him to the West Indies. She served in the army for many years, even getting a bayonet wound in her arm at the Battle of Fontenoy. She never told anyone she was a girl until her man was wounded and sent to hospital. She told the General's wife and was allowed to follow and nurse him. For years she kept a fruit & veg stall near the Steine and was well known in the city. She was friends with the Prince Regent who called her "a jolly good fellow" and gave her a pension of eighteen pounds a year and paid the stone cutter who made her gravestone when she eventually popped her clogs.

There is also a graveyard in Hove, just opposite the library. In here you will find the grave of Welshman

Sir George Everest, the Surveyor General of India from 1823-1843. He was very meticulous in getting together all of the information to calculate the height of the mountains of the Himalayas. As a result the highest mountain in the world was named in his honour, Mount Everest.

The Old Lanes / North Laine

Finally you've got the Lanes. Voted the second coolest place in Britain (don't know who by but probably very important style gurus!), they must be visited. Of course the shops are great but so are the cafés, street performers and the general sights and sounds. Just hang around and soak in the atmosphere - looking out for ghosts of course!

Hanging Out - With The Rich And Famous

Brighton & Hove is well known as a place full of the rich and famous. Celebrities from all over the world have ended up in Brighton & Hove on a permanent basis and many more come to visit.

In the Brunswick area there are lots of little blue plaques commemorating the people from many years ago; it is quite interesting just to wander around and see who was around and about and what they were achieving. There is also a 'Walk of Fame' in the Marina, supposed to be like the pavement in Hollywood, featuring 45 famous celebrities that have an association with the city.

DID YOU KNOW?

That Winston Churchill, the Prime Minister during the 2nd World War went to school in Hove for a short while?

Local buses have the names of famous residents past and present on the front, see if there is anyone you recognise. There is definitely a 'Fat Boy Slim' aka Norman Cook out there as well as a few more obscure ones like Harry Cowley who was a chimney sweep who fought for workers rights. There is a story behind everyone, find out more from the buses website. In terms of more up to date celebrities you do see a few of these around town too.

> **DID YOU KNOW?**
> The amazing Swedish super group Abba won the 1974 Eurovision Song Contest in the Brighton Dome with the song 'Waterloo', kick starting their popularity. Get a grown up to sing it for you!

Chris Eubank, the infamous boxer with a lisp is often posing around in his huge truck or in his flash jeep. He makes no attempt to disguise himself, appearing to love the attention. He'll definitely be open to an autograph.

Zoë Ball the radio DJ and Fat Boy Slim the eminent DJ and Record Producer live in a huge house with their own private beach by Hove Lagoon. They generally keep themselves to themselves but Zoë does shop on the Western Rd.

Sir Paul McCartney and Heather Mills also own a house on the so called 'Millionaires Row' next door to Zoë and the Fat Boy as does Nick Berry of Heartbeat and Eastenders fame; ask your mum if you've never heard of him.

> What do you call a man who can sing and drink lemonade at the same time? A pop singer!

Aged pop star David Van Day(from the '80's group Dollar) used to serve burgers and chips from his mobile van up by Churchill Square, but you don't seem to see him around so much now that there is a kind of 1980's pop revival going on.

Leo Sayer, another golden oldie is a local, again your parents might be able to sing one of his songs.

HANGING OUT

Comedian extraordinaire Steve Coogan lives in Hove, he can often be seen on Church Road pottering about.

Steve Ovett and Sally Gunnel (Olympic runners) both have local connections. Steve went to Varndean School and the Art College and his dad had a greengrocery stall in the market by The Level, whilst Sally still lives in the area.

Emma Bunton from the Spice Girls apparently has a flat on the sea front.

When it is the Party in the Park in June every year loads of stars stay in the Grand Hotel, a good place to hang out and celebrity spot. Bands playing at the Brighton Centre also stay there as it is right next door.

Hanging Out - Shopping

Brighton & Hove has a number of different areas that are good for different kinds of shopping.

Shopping Areas

The Old Lanes

The Old Lanes are famous for jewellery shops, from your normal everyday chain stores to specialist antique jewellery shops, designer silverware shops and other original and unusual creations like the armour shop. You can find things that are a real bargain or you can spend serious amounts of cash.

TOP 5 WEIRDEST SHOPS
- Vegetarian Shoe Shop
- Heavy Petting Dog Accessory Shop
- The Lanes Armoury
- ChoccyWoccyDooDah Chocolate Shop
- Snooper's Paradise Flea Market

There are also lots of other little arty shops, great for birthday and Christmas presents, as well as cafés to hang out in.

North Laine
The North Laine area is similar but different. The shops here are completely out of the ordinary (being polite). This is where you go when you want something unusual and you've tried everywhere else. From vegetarian shoes to vegan pastries and juggling balls to multi-coloured beads; you can find them all here. Well worth a wander around, but don't go too early on a Sunday, lots of shops don't open until after 11am or even 12pm!

Churchill Square
For your every day chain stores and banks go to Churchill Square and nearby Western Road and North Street. Churchill Square is an indoor shopping complex with 84 shops and a food court, a good place to shop if it is raining!

Kemptown
Kemptown is the area from Old Steine up to the Marina. The main shopping area is St James Street leading up to St Georges Road. As well as normal shops like Safeway and Boots there are a few unusual shops here too, like second hand books and antique shops, a shop specialising in Dolls Houses and miniature furniture (The Mulberry Bush) and a hairdressers and accessory shop for dogs. Bizarre!

Brighton Marina
Brighton Marina is growing and developing all of the time. As well as a big Asda, cinema and bowling alley there are quite a few designer outlet stores giving good discounts on clothes, books, shoes and handbags. If you get hungry there is a family friendly pub, a some really nice restaurants and a McDonalds. Parking here is free.

Hove
Church Street and George Street are the main shopping areas in Hove. Like other places in the area you

will find a combination of the High Street favourites alongside small unusual boutiques and cafés and restaurants.

Markets
Brighton has a big market / car boot sale every Sunday in the station car park. It sells all sorts of clothes, antiques, toys, food, plants - you name it and it'll be there. On London Road there is the Open Market (renowned for fruit and vegetables) and in Kemptown there is the Flea Market. This doesn't sell fleas and you don't get fleas if you go there; so who knows why it is called a Flea Market! Anyway, it's full of old stuff.

> What do you call it when a flea kills itself? Insecticide!!

The guide below helps you if there is something specific you are after.

Clothes Shops
There are loads of clothes shops in Brighton and we just can't go through them all, so instead we have covered them by area.

The **North Laine** is full of interesting but unusual clothes shops...try out 'Cutie', 'Rockit' and 'Ju Ju'. 'Immediate Clothing' in Sydney Street mainly has old vintage gear, but they also do some smart T-shirts. If you skate, check out 'One 40 Five' also on Sydney Street, it has lots of 'Stüssy' as well as 'Holmes', 'Freshjive' and 'addict' - very cool brands. Across the road, about half way down North Street is 'TK Maxx', good for designer clothes or unusual gear at a good price.

Western Road, just opposite Churchill Square, has 'Top Shop', 'Etam', 'New Look' and 'Primark' right next to each other for a huge shopfest. Fashion sports shops like 'JJB Sport', 'JD Sport', 'Footlocker' and 'Allsports' are also around Churchill Square.

Inside the **Churchill Square** complex itself you will find 'Next', 'River Island', 'Dorothy Perkins' and 'Debenhams'. If you are really girly and pink is your favourite colour you will like 'Claire's Accessories'.

Arty Crafty Stuff

Brighton is full of little arty shops with all kinds of bits and pieces to decorate you or your bedroom or to give as presents. The best of these are in the Lanes.

Cissy Mo
✉ 38 Sydney Street, North Laine, Brighton and 25 Church Road, Hove
☎ 01273 607777

This shop has the most bizarre collection of stuff, from fur trimmed rubber gloves and fish covered toilet seats to hilarious birthday cards and mini table football games. Lots of pink things here too.

Tsena
✉ 6 Bond Street, North Laine, Brighton
☎ 01273 328402

It is quite expensive here, but it has beautiful, special and unique presents. Worth a little look around even if you are not going to buy anything.

England at Home
✉ 22 & 32 Ship Street in the Old Lanes, Brighton
☎ 01273 205544

These shops are just down the road from TK Maxx. The little one on the corner has lots of bits and pieces, again ideal for presents.

Beads Unlimited
✉ 21 Sydney Street, North Laine, Brighton
☎ 01273 675077

Another delightful shop on Sydney Street where you can find millions of beads in all shapes, sizes and colours. Think of all of the unique jewellery you could make. There are other shops nearby selling fun fabric and craft tools and accessories.

Scrumptious Shops

Brighton Rock Shop
✉ 42 Kings Road, Brighton
☎ 01273 327740

For good old traditional seaside rock, go to the Brighton Rock Shop on the seafront. They have the favourite pink stuff with 'Brighton' right the way through it, and even stuff with your name on it (unless your name is Ethelred or Cloud, they are a bit too unusual). You can also get sugar false teeth, dummies and a few other ruder items to embarrass your granny!

What do you call someone with a massive bag of sweets? Your new best mate!

Choccywoccydoodah
✉ 27a, Middle St, Old Lanes, Brighton
☎ 01273 329462

This is where you will find the most drool-worthy cakes in the whole planet. You can almost smell the chocolate as you walk up the street. It's worth just going in to look at the cakes, enormous confections with lavish swirls of thick, rich, dark chocolate embellished with ribbons and bows. Truly mouth-watering. They also do truffles, special chocolate bars and moulded chocolate, things like bunnies and eggs at Easter and allsorts at Christmas.

Montezumas Chocolates
✉ 15 Duke St, Old Lanes, Brighton
☎ 01273 324 979

Another chocolate lover's paradise. This place has delicious, handmade chocolates, made just down the road in Chichester with high quality chocolate made from cocoa beans from the Dominican Republic. It is also very right on, with GM-free and organic products in recycled and reusable packaging, altogether highly ethical.

ShakeAway

✉ 8 Bond Street, North Laine, Brighton
☎ 01273 711179

You have got to go here. Get your mitts on the must have accessory, a blue and yellow ShakeAway cup full of a delicious milkshake concoction devised by your very good self. Have whatever you fancy; Toblerone, Honey, Banana and Popcorn maybe, or perhaps you might prefer something a little fruity like Strawberry, Passion Fruit and Jelly Tots? On average it takes customers 4.47 minutes to pick what they want - there is just so much to choose from. Collect 10 stamps on your Cow Card and you get a free milkshake.

Sports Shops

Churchill Square has all of the usual sports shops like JJB Sports and Foot Locker. Brighton & Hove also have a few specialist sports shops.

RUN

✉ 46 Blatchington Road, Hove
☎ 01273 770972

If you are a serious runner then this is one of the best shops in the land. The guys are runners themselves so they are very knowledgeable and will spend time with you to make sure you get the right shoes and any other running related equipment.

Airborne Kites

✉ 42 Gardner Street, North Laine, Brighton
☎ 01273 676740

This has got to be one of the best kite shops ever, the people here know everything you need to know about flying all kinds of kites and sports associated with it like kite surfing and kite buggying. You won't believe the number of colours, shapes and designs - a great birthday present.

Oddballs
✉ 24 Kensington Gardens, North Laine, Brighton
☎ 01273 696068

This shop sells kites, roller blades, roller skates, skate boards, juggling balls; well all kinds of fun things really. They also have a hire shop down on the Seafront, by the old West Pier.

ODDBALL BONUS
The best bit about Oddballs is that many of the big cost things come with a 28 day money back guarantee so if you get bored / don't use them / they feel uncomfortable then you can take them back. This goes down really well with the parents if they won't let you get what you want as they don't believe you will use it. Prove you will use it or they can take it back and everyone's happy!

Re-Al
✉ 7 Dukes Lane, Old Lanes, Brighton
☎ 01273 325658

The place to go for all skateboard clothing and equipment. Loads of cool stuff sold by cool people who know what is hot and what is not.

Ocean Sports Board Riders
✉ 368 Kingsway, Hove.
☎ 01273 412241

You have do go way down in deepest, darkest Hove to find this place, although it is very handy if you are Fat Boy Slim or Paul McCartney. The name is a bit of a giveaway, they have everything for snow boarding, kite boarding and surfboarding and claim to have the 'best prices in the UK'.

David Rose Sports
✉ 41 Western Rd, Hove
☎ 01273 326362

This is a 'proper' sports shop that actually sells bats, balls, cues and sticks as well as clothes and shoes. The people in here also know what they are talking about; a good place to go if you are serious about Cricket, Rugby, Football, Hockey, Tennis etc. They also know about local sports clubs.

Sydney Street Bikes
✉ 24 Sydney Street, North Laine, Brighton
☎ 01273 624700

This place comes highly recommended for great service as well as great bikes - all the best names for mountain bikes and BMX. They have another shop on Portland Rd in Hove.

Action Bikes
✉ 93 London Road, Brighton
☎ 01273 605160

This has a good selection of kid's bikes and does workshops on looking after your bike and quick repairs. They are part of a big chain so can usually get good prices. Their catch phrase is a bit corny... 'the bike chain that won't let you down'; good try but not funny!

Games Shops

The obvious places to buy games are shops like Game, HMV, WH Smith and Virgin in Churchill Square and along Western Road. The change around in these kind of shops is amazing, they are there one week and gone the next so much as we try to be accurate we can't guarantee these will all be around.

There is an ace second hand game shop in Sydney Street in the North Laine, where you can pick up old computer and console games.

Magazine and Comic Shops

For current magazines you can't beat WH Smith or Borders in Churchill Square.

For something more unusual try David's Comic Shop on Sydney Street.

Reservoir Frogs in Kensington Gardens, North Laine has been described as 'the best comic shop in the South-East' selling more unusual comics. Worth a visit if you like that sort of thing.

Hanging Out - Sports

Outdoor Sports

Boarding / BMX / Blading

There are a few good places to hang out as Brighton was one of the first skating hot spots in the country. Unbelievably the local council support skating and even has a skate strategy. They also consult with skaters in developing new facilities.

The latest development is an indoor skate park at Brighton Youth Centre. You don't even need your own equipment here as you can hire everything, but everyone has to wear a helmet, so if you don't have one be prepared to borrow one. Older, experienced skaters are on hand to give guidance and coaching; there

UNOFFICIAL LOCAL SKATE SPOTS

- There are quite a few spots along the front between the piers and in the old paddling pool. This is really popular at weekends and in the school holidays.
- The Esplanade is a popular hang-out by Hove Lawns. You can even have skate lessons, by yourself or with others. Call 07931 381265 or check out the link at www.knapsackguides.com.
- Bartholomew Square is popular, around Moshi Moshi Sushi.
- The covered car park under the Sainsburys on Lewes Road attracts skaters as it has kerbs, humps and bumps to try out your tricks.
- The car park at the Brighton & Hove Sixth Form College (BHASVIC) has tough ledges but you might have to pass as a student!
- BUT, don't annoy people (well not to much anyway!). Skaters and skateboarders can easily get a bad reputation by abusing private property or causing an obstruction. It's fine to enjoy yourself, just don't spoil it for everyone else. That's the end of the lecture!

TOP 5 OUTDOOR SPORTS

- Swimming in the Sea
- Skateboarding / BMX at the Level
- Kiting at Stanmer Park
- Football on Hove Lawns
- Roller skating along the Esplanade

are also first-aiders so if you come a cropper they can help you out! Telephone 01273 681368 for more information. [Note - aimed at 10-16 year olds].

There is also a purpose-built outdoor skate park with lots of verts, ramps, pipes, boxes and ledges up at the Level, just up and across from the Pavilions. This is unsupervised and without first-aiders. There are other local authority sites at Black Rock, Woodingdean, Knoll Recreation Ground and Preston Park. These are intended for a range of ages and abilities, from beginners to proficient skaters and have lots of steel and concrete structures to do tricks galore.

There are also plans to build five other skate parks including one at Hove Lagoon.

Kiting

The seaside is a great place to fly a kite, but so is the countryside. Luckily you can do both in Brighton & Hove. Both the beach and Hove Lawns are great places to fly kites, as long as you are careful and don't smash the kite down on the unsuspecting sunbathers below. Stanmer Park and Devil's Dyke are brilliant countryside venues.

Every year in July there is a huge Kite Festival at Stanmer Park. It has been taking place for over 25 years and hundreds of people from all over the UK and abroad make their way to show off their kites and their flying skills. You can learn how to make kites as well as fly them yourself and enjoy the other entertainment that is there, such as kite fighting competitions.

Mini Golf / Pitch & Putt

There are a few places to go to if you are a golf fan. There is a crazy golf place on Madeira Drive that is quite good but not very high tech and a very tiny one in Hove by the King Alfred Sports Centre. There are putting greens in most of the parks which are well maintained if not very exciting.

For serious golf fans the best places to go are the Pitch and Putt courses along the sea front towards Rottingdean. There is a nine hole course next to Rodean school and a hilly 18 hole course by the Rottingdean windmill. Both are quite difficult and give fantastic views over the sea. Great fun on a sunny day!

Riding

Funnily enough there aren't any riding schools in the middle of the city centre, but there are a few in the countryside not too far away. If you are a riding fan then call up the stables listed below, each are very child friendly and will be very keen to help:

- ✉ Rottingdean Riding School, Chailey Avenue, Rottingdean
- ☎ 01273 302155
- ✉ Three Greys Riding School, Clayton Hill, Pyecombe Nr Brighton
- ☎ 01273 843536

Swimming

- ✉ Saltdean Lido, Saltdean Park Road, Saltdean
- ☎ 01273 305155

If you fancy swimming outside then pop on down to the lido at Saltdean. As well as being good fun it is also a piece of history, places like this were very fashionable in the 'Art Deco' period of the 1930's. You can tell this by the style of the buildings and the decorations. It gets dead busy on sunny days, so probably best to get there early.

Stoolball
Have you heard of stoolball? It is a bit like a cross between rounders and cricket and one of the oldest games around, played since 1450 and mentioned in the famous book 'Don Quixote'. Sussex is one of the few places left in Britain where stoolball is still played and there is a thriving league.

Tennis
Many of the parks have tennis courts. There are also tennis courts at the Withdean Sports Complex and towards Hove Lagoon (pay fee at the King Alfred Centre). They always seem to be busiest around Wimbledon fortnight in June when it can be hard to get a court. In October every year the Brighton Centre hosts the top level Brighton International Ladies Tennis Championship.

Why don't fish play tennis? 'Cos they get caught up in the net!

Watersports
✉ Hove Lagoon, Kingsway, Hove
☎ 01273 424842

This is the place to learn to windsurf, sail a dinghy, canoe, surf, ski or build a raft. Really exciting stuff! It's also quite safe 'cos the water is only waist deep and the instructors are all properly qualified. They only let you in if you are over eight and you can't go in the power-boat or on the banana ride unless you are over twelve, but there are loads of other things to do if you are in between. All of the equipment is there to hire and the instructors will help you whether you are a complete beginner or if you've done stuff before. They hold fantastic activity weeks during the school holidays.

Hanging Out

53

Indoor Sports

The city has loads of leisure centres, swimming pools and a bowling alley as well as many sports clubs and societies. Whether you are a swimmer, a gymnast or if you play squash or table tennis, there is somewhere for you to go.

King Alfred Leisure Centre
✉ Kingsway, Hove
☎ 01273 290290

This is the largest leisure centre in the city but it has grand plans for redevelopment, so it might not be there by the time you visit! At the time of writing it had a couple of swimming pools with slides and bridges and a huge sports hall for 5-A-Side Football, Badminton, Volleyball, Basketball and Table Tennis as well as a Gym. It also runs quite a few good classes. The new leisure centre promises to be even better, but it won't be around until at least 2006!

Prince Regent Swimming Pool
✉ Church Street, Brighton
☎ 01273 685692

This swimming pool complex has 4 pools (including a learning pool) and is right in the middle of town, quite near the Pavilion. It is home to the Brighton Swimming Club, the oldest swimming club in England which has been around since 1860. The club was started by a group of mad guys who regularly met to swim in the sea by the Palace Pier. Many still do this, especially on Christmas Day! The Prince Regent Swimming Pool has a deep water diving pool for diving and for synchronised swimming (also known as aquatic dancing!), it's getting quite trendy you know since it became an Olympic sport. You can also play water polo, have swimming les-

> **DID YOU KNOW?**
> Do you know why Water Polo is called Water Polo? Well, when it was first played in 1870 the men used to ride on barrels in the water (a bit like horses) and would hit the ball with a mallet just like in normal polo. So there you go!

sons or join the Brighton Swimming Club itself and take part in galas and competitions.

Stanley Deason Leisure Centre
✉ Wilson Avenue, Brighton
☎ 01273 694281

This is quite a small sports centre on the edge of town with a multi-purpose sports hall, a gym for grown ups, some squash courts and two all weather football/hockey pitches.

St Luke's Swimming Pool
✉ St. Luke's Terrace, Brighton
☎ 01273 602385

This has a mini pool (well small, but not paddling pool size!) and a training pool for general swimming and lessons. You can hire out the pool for parties - could be good for a birthday treat.

Moulsecoomb Community Sports Centre
✉ Moulescoomb Way, Brighton
☎ 01273 622266

A bit similar to Stanley Deason, this has a large sports hall and a fitness area. More for grown ups!

Withdean Sports Complex
✉ Tongdean Lane, Withdean, Brighton
☎ 01273 542100

This indoor and outdoor complex is home to the Brighton & Hove Albion Football Club and has a fantastic outdoor athletics track with excellent facilities for the resident Brighton and Hove Athletics Club. There are also facilities for American Football, indoor and outdoor tennis, squash and dance and fitness. Quite a combination.

DID YOU KNOW?

Olympic gold medallist Steve Ovett started his athletics career at the Brighton and Hove Athletics Club, in fact he still holds the club record for 400m, 800m, 1500m, 3000m and 5000m, not bad eh? They welcome new members and have a really good standard of athletes including a few who are no.1 in the UK in their event.

HANGING OUT

Bowlplex
✉ Brighton Marina
☎ 01273 818180
£ from £2.95 - £4.95

Brighton Marina's award winning ten-pin bowling complex has all that you would expect of a modern bowling centre, with pool tables, video games and a food place as well as the bowling itself. There are 26 lanes and it is quite easy to book. They have lots of light balls that you can help yourself to and they have the special ramps to make them easy to bowl. You can also get inflatable cushions put down the gulleys to keep your ball going in the right direction.

DID YOU KNOW?
Primitive bowling implements, consisting of 9 pieces of stone and a stone ball were found in an Egyptian tomb buried with a child in 5200BC BC.

Watching sport

Brighton & Hove can be a great place to watch sport. With a great, well supported Football Team; one of the UK's best basketball teams and a County and International Cricket Ground, you are spoilt for choice.

Brighton & Hove Albion
✉ Withdean Stadium
☎ 01273 776992

The Second Division Seagulls have a huge following in the town, with Fat Boy Slim being a big supporter. Home matches are very exciting and the town becomes covered in blue and white. For young supporters under sixteen there is the 'Seagulls Club'. You pay to join and get a club t-shirt and a discount in the shop for other goodies, the chance to be ball girl / boy and the team mascot, a photo of the team or your fave player, ticket priority, birthday and Christmas cards and a regular Newsletter. You can also play in their

Why was the football pitch soggy? Because the players were always dribbling!

youth team or do 5-a-side training. They have everything a football fan could possibly want.

Brighton Bears
- ✉ The Brighton Centre, Kings Road, Brighton
- ☎ 01273 6266943
- £ Kids £6 (Adults £10, Family £28)

The Brighton Bears are one of the best basketball teams in the country. The Brighton Centre hosts their Brighton home games; an exciting frenzy of on court tricks and tribulations. Each games lasts just 40 minutes, divided into four quarters of 10 minutes each, with loads of entertainment in the breaks. The evening is fun packed with dancing cheerleaders, mexican waves and groovy booming music from Southern FM. Have a go at the dribbling and shooting competitions and the 'chuck a duck' throw-in, with the chance to win balls and Bears memorabilia. It really is an unforgettable night out.

Sussex County Cricket Ground
- ✉ Eaton Road, Hove.
- ☎ 01273 827100

The Sussex Sharks play at Hove and at Arundel. County matches and International's are both held at Hove and are a great way to spend a sunny afternoon. Courses for all abilities, with English Cricket Board qualified coaches, are held for kids all through the year. You can also get junior membership of the Sussex County Cricket Club which gives access to Members' facilities, priority booking for knock-out cup matches, half price Club Handbooks and a discount on the excellent coaching courses. Junior Gold membership also gives you the chance to be a mascot for NCL matches.

What job did Dracula do for his local cricket team? He looked after the bats!

Greyhound Racing

✉ Coral Brighton & Hove Stadium, Nevill Road, Hove.

☎ 01273 204601

ⓘ open : 6:30pm-11pm Tue, Thu, Sat; 2:30pm-5pm Wed, Sun

> **DID YOU KNOW?**
>
> Greyhounds are a really old breed of dog, even getting a mention in the Bible.
>
> Greyhound racing is the second biggest spectator sport in the UK. Standard races are 515m in distance, the record holder for this distance is Windgap Java who ran it in 29.56 seconds

This might not sound like the most exciting night out but it can be fun, honestly! Hove Racecourse is also one of the best and fastest in the UK. It is free to go on Wednesday afternoons and Sunday Lunchtimes and they have special deals the rest of the time. Watch the speedy greyhounds chase the poor little fluffy bunny round the track, whilst old geezers bet their last few pennies. Get an adult to put a little bet on trap 3 on the 3rd race, you never know, it might win! The place has been refurbished but it is still a little bit seedy, a good place to go if you fancy something different.

Horse Racing

✉ Brighton Racecourse, Freshfield Road, Brighton

☎ 01273 603580

£ FREE! for kids

If you like horses then you might fancy going horse racing - and it's free for kids. Brighton racecourse is high up

> Where do Jockeys go on holiday? Horse-tria!

in the hills behind the city where you get a wonderful view across the South Downs and the English Channel. The racing itself can be quite exciting. As it is quite a small racecourse you get to be close to the action, but it can be hard to see the race amongst all of the tall, over excited grown ups. It is also worth watching the beautiful, shining horses and stroppy mini jockeys strut around the parade ring before the races start. A good time to go is on the Family Sunday events in the summer that are more geared up for kids.

Hanging Out - Cultural and Arty Stuff

Discovering Stuff

Brighton Museum and Art Gallery
- Pavilion Gardens, Brighton.
- 01273 290900
- Open Mon-Sat 10am-5pm, Sunday 2-5pm. Closed Weds, most BH's.
- £ FREE!

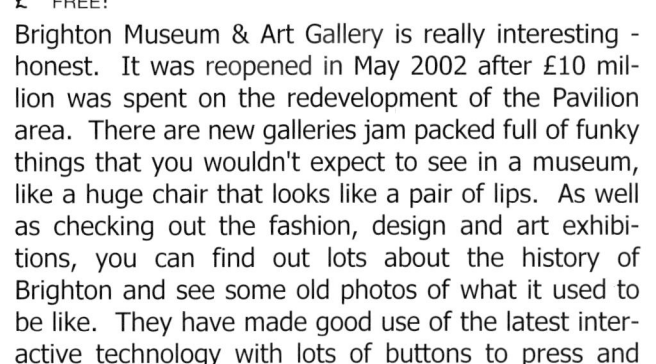

Brighton Museum & Art Gallery is really interesting - honest. It was reopened in May 2002 after £10 million was spent on the redevelopment of the Pavilion area. There are new galleries jam packed full of funky things that you wouldn't expect to see in a museum, like a huge chair that looks like a pair of lips. As well as checking out the fashion, design and art exhibitions, you can find out lots about the history of Brighton and see some old photos of what it used to be like. They have made good use of the latest interactive technology with lots of buttons to press and speaker things to listen to; real stories from real people. During the school holidays the museum holds all kinds of kids' workshops.

Hove Museum and Art Gallery
- 19 New Church Road, Hove.
- 01273 290200
- Open Tues-Sat 10am-5pm, Sun 2-5pm. Closed BHs
- £ FREE!

Hove Museum reopened in 2003 after an £800,000 refurbishment; enough to buy 2.5 million bags of crisps - imagine that. Instead of buying crisps they have created a 'Wizard's Attic' full of toys from Queen Victoria's time right up to Barbie Dolls. It is one of the biggest and best toy collections in the whole of Britain. As this was one of the starting places for film making (the close-up and the editing process were both invented here) there is also a Film Gallery. Lots to see and play about with, well worth a visit on a rainy day! It also has lots of great activities during the school holidays.

Fabrica
- 40 Duke Street, Old Lanes, Brighton
- 01273 778646
- FREE!

Now this place has some really weird stuff in it, but worth a look as you walk by. Right in the middle of the Old Lanes is a groovy old church that has been converted into a gallery showing bizarre art. From delicate structures made of string and plastic to exhibitions where you become part of the art; you won't have seen anything like it.

Booth Museum of Natural History
- 194 Dyke Road, Brighton
- 01273 292777
- Open 10am- 5pm; Sun 2 - 5pm. Closed Thurs & BHs
- FREE!

This place really is bizarre but fascinating. There are over half a million 'specimens' from up to 300 years ago - stuffed birds, butterflies, skeletons and odd bones. It is a bit dark and dingy inside; but this kind of adds to the atmosphere.

Watching & Doing Stuff

The Brighton Dome
- Church Street, Brighton
- 01273 700747

The Dome includes the Pavilion Theatre and Corn Exchange and has great facilities for concerts, conferences, art exhibitions, dance and opera. It holds some fantastic productions for kids as well as dancing every Monday afternoon and occasional special events like Stage Fighting Workshops. Worth checking out.

The Theatre Royal
✉ New Road, Brighton
☎ 01273 328488

Theatreland is concentrated around the North Laine with the Theatre Royal at its centre. It's a grand old theatre (first curtain call was 'Hamlet' in 1807) with a beautiful auditorium. It holds family and children's shows throughout out the year with a pantomime at Christmas of course, usually starring someone from Neighbours or a Big Brother reject!

The Duke of York's Cinema
✉ Preston Circus, Brighton
☎ 01273 602503
ⓘ Every Saturday Morning

Junior Dukes takes place on Saturdays and is well wicked. It only costs £3 a year for membership and you get into any of the films for only £2 (£2.50 non members). Not only that you also get invitations to special events, a quarterly newsletter and you get to go to the cinema on your birthday for a trip to the projection box, a present and a card. Best of all grown ups can only come if they are accompanied by a child so it's clear who rules here. Aside from Saturdays it is quite a serious place with lots of foreign and arty films; might not be quite up your street.

Komedia
✉ Gardner St, North Laine, Brighton
☎ 01273 647100
ⓘ Sunday afternoons

Right in the middle of the cool North Laine you will find Komedia, a trendy theatre voted one of the best family friendly venues in the South East. On Sundays they have shows for kids (from 3+ so some may be a little young for you). They have lots of other school holiday activities that you can get involved in.

The Brighton Centre

✉ Kings Road, Brighton
☎ 01273 290131

When it's not home to the annual party conferences and a host of other functions, the Brighton Centre is the place to see Blazing Squad, Atomic Kitten or the latest Pop Idol sensation. Situated along the seafront just up from the Pier it is also the stage for the Holiday on Ice extravaganzas and home to the Brighton Bears Basketball team.

Hanging Out - Nosh

Global Adventure!

You can eat almost anything in Brighton & Hove depending on how adventurous you are feeling, it can also be a real experience, much more than just eating food. People have come to Brighton & Hove from all over the world and some have set up restaurants serving their native foods, a real global kitchen. We have listed some great places below, they not only serve good food, they are also especially welcoming and fun for kids in terms of the meals and the place itself.

TOP 5 FUN PLACES TO EAT OUT
- Dig in the Ribs
- Moshi Moshi Sushi
- Shakeaway (well drink anyway!)
- Cactus Canteen
- One of the places on the Pier

Seafront Grub

The seafront cafés are perfect for grabbing a bite on a sunny afternoon; you can get quite a variety from the traditional fish and chips to pizza, burgers, BBQ's and things a little healthier like salads and seafood.

Get into the Lanes

For something a bit more substantial or a bit more glamorous in the evening The Old Lanes has everything you could ask for; from the chains like ASK and

Pizza Express to Italian joints to French bistros, Spanish tapas bars, Mexican restaurants and steak houses. You name it and it's probably there! Almost every street you walk up will have some sort of restaurant so you won't get hungry!

Unchained...
We haven't included the big chain restaurants as they are all here and aren't especially different or exciting. If you want to go somewhere you know and you can depend on, then of course these places are great. They can be found around the main shopping area (Western Road / North Road and the North Laine). But they are very samey and not terribly adventurous, the places on the next page, are all a little bit unusual or especially kid friendly.

Your Restaurant Reviews
Don't forget to look at the latest restaurant reviews on www.knapsackguides.com; there are pictures of many of the places and of the menus. If you visit a cool eatery and you

YUCCKKKKK
This food tastes of soap!!!
Well, at least you know the kitchens are clean!!!

have a comment to make we want to hear from you, please write to us at grubsup@knapsackguides.com and we'll put it up on the site.

Cafés and Restaurants

Alfresco
✉ The Milkmaid Pavilion, King's Road Arches, Brighton.
☎ 01273 206523

The best bit about this place is the location; it's right on the seafront opposite the site of the West Pier. In the summer they have loads of tables and chairs out side so that you really can eat 'al fresco' (in the open air). It is a great Italian serving lovely pasta and pizza as well as quite posh meat and fish dishes. They don't have special kid's meals, you just get to pick from the proper menu. Proper grown up stuff for a special occasion.

Bankers Fish and Chip Restaurant
✉ 116a Western Rd, Brighton.
☎ 01273 328267

Ok so this place looks quite old and it has probably seen better days, but it does serve the best fish and chips so you can't complain. It is a very traditional British Chippy; you can take away your fish and chips, but you can't beat sitting in the restaurant. Now you can imagine what is was like eating out when your Granny was your age. Have cod and chips and mushy peas with lots of salt and vinegar, lip-smacking gorgeous!

What is all that rubbish doing in the restaurant? Someone left a tip!

The Boardwalk
✉ 250a Kings Road Arches, Brighton
☎ 01273 746067

The best thing about Boardwalk is the location, right by the Palace Pier with views over the sea. As a consequence they get dead busy in the summer so you need to get there early. They have a huge outdoor eating area where you can sit out in the summer. The food is good value tasty but healthy stuff and they have some interesting soft drinks and juices. Good toilets!

Browns
✉ 3-4 Duke Street, Brighton
☎ 01273 323501

Another quite posh and actually quite trendy place. Chris Eubank has been seen (you know, the old boxer bloke with a lisp) outside here a few times. This is a nice place to go with really good service, just sit at the table and wait to be served. They do have a special kid's menu and you even get free ice cream - how's that for a good deal?

Cactus Canteen

✉ 5 Bright Square, Brighton.
☎ 01273 725700

Have you tried proper Mexican food before? This is a good place to try it as it does a combination of stuff from burgers to burritos, so if you're a bit nervous about trying the Mexican food order yourself a big juicy Texan burger and then try everyone else's more adventurous stuff. Sound like a plan? This is also quite a fun and lively place with fake cacti and bright colours everywhere.

China Garden

✉ 88 Preston Street, Brighton
☎ 01273 325124

Massive Chinese restaurant with terrible décor but fab food that makes up for it. Lots of people say how good this place is; the food really is apparently fantastic (try the mixed hors d'oeurves platter to start) and the service cannot be faulted even if you come

RESTAURANT TRICKS!

Try these tricks in restaurants - they are sure to impress NOT!

- Call the waiter over by clicking your fingers above your head.
- Burp loudly and smack your lips after every course and say 'Corrrr, lovely'.
- Tuck your napkin into the top of your shirt, make it look as stupid as possible.
- Ask for an explanation of all of the complicated fancy stuff on the menu and then order something really obvious and simple.
- Ask if you can have your drink with ice, a slice and an umbrella.

in a big group. Might be a good place to suggest for a grown up's birthday treat. They don't let very little kids in and they don't have a kid's menu - big kid stuff!! Get a seat by the window for great sea views.

HANGING

The Cuthbert
✉ Freshfield Road, Brighton
☎ 01273 680673

A real family-orientated pub with kids really welcome in the beer garden. In the summer they even let you use the barbecue completely free of charge (well the grown ups, but you can supervise!). Just bring your own food and your own charcoal and you've got it made.

OUT

Devil's Dyke Pub
✉ Devil's Dyke, Poynings
☎ 01273 857256

This is a great place to eat if you have been watching the paragliders or if you have been for a walk around Devil's Dyke. It is one of the pub chains, but it does serve a good Sunday lunch and has a Kid's menu with the usual chicken nuggets and fish fingers. You can also sit outside and take in the rays on a sunny day.

Dig in the Ribs
✉ 47 Preston Street, Brighton
☎ 01273 325275

Tex-mex is really gorgeous and very popular and there are few better places to try it than this funky and happening joint. They really welcome kids but you need to book in advance so they can get things ready for you. They have a great 'Kids Grits' Menu with entertaining food like 'Prairies Dog' 'Goldfish Toes' and 'Smack-in-the-chops Sauce' and 'Buffalo Fries'. The perfect place for a birthday treat as they make you feel very special, putting balloons up for you and singing 'Happy Birthday To You'. A little embarrassing but worth it!

TOP 5 PLACES TO EAT OUTDOORS

- Alfresco, Seafront
- The Boardwalk, Seafront
- The Dorset, North Laine
- Lucy's Restaurant, Seafront
- Get some fish and chips and eat them on the beach

Donatello
✉ Brighton Place, Old Lanes, Brighton
☎ 01273 775477

This is just so family friendly that it is completely full of kids of all ages - great in terms of the welcome but maybe not so great if you don't fancy being surrounded by 3 year olds. It is really, really popular as it does tasty Italian food at good value prices. Pasta is especially cheap, they do kid's portions (that are still huge) for only £3. It is also popular with the rich and famous - Tony Blair has even eaten here during the Labour Party Conference; there are loads of pictures of the owners with their celebrity guests.

The Dorset
✉ 28 North Road, North Laine, Brighton
☎ 01273605423

This is a café/ pub/restaurant open for delicious breakfasts, scrummy lunches then turns into a pub in the evening. It lets you guys in until 8pm, plenty of time to soak up the atmosphere of this very Brighton place. It is in a great location in the middle of the North Laine; if you can get an outside table it is a fab place just to people watch - you'll see a wide range of bizarre characters!

English's
✉ 29-31 East Street, Brighton
☎ 01273 3279808

So how brave are you when it comes to fish, real fish (so no fancy shapes or fingers!)? Ever eaten an oyster? Mussels? Squid? This is the place to try such delicacies if you

DID YOU KNOW?
- Oysters have little hearts which pump colourless blood!
- There are male and female oysters, and they can change from one to the other!!

dare... this is also quite a quaint little place in the Old Lanes, quite higgledy-piggledy; you can imagine that it has been around for years. It is supposed to have the best seafood in Brighton so if fish is your thing this is the place to go.

Food For Friends
✉ 17 Prince Albert Street, Old Lanes, Brighton
☎ 01273 202310

You will find all kinds of people in 'Food For Friends', old grannies, hippy types, students and people like you. It's a vegetarian place with quite a good selection of daily changing hot dishes like pastas and stir-fries as well as a choice of interesting salads. You'll feel very good and very wholesome if you go here.

MEAL TIME FUN!

Have some fun with your food, who says meal times should be serious?
- Mash potato is a great material for sculpture or for decorating with other vegetables to create a truly unique piece of art.
- Mash potato is also a great place to hide nasty chewy bits of meat or soggy veg.
- Pop something like some peas or some noodles into the pocket of a grown-ups coat, I'm sure they will laugh when they find it later!! NOT!
- Get an ice cream soda, quietly blow bubbles into it, and watch it grow.
- Take a little plastic bug or spider with you; slip it on to your sister's plate.
- Create a tower, pile all your food on top of each other in a huge stack, it's what all of the top chefs do you know.

The George
✉ 5 Trafalgar St, Brighton
☎ 01273 681055

The George is quite a big pub with a beer garden, serves vegetarian food, with some vegan dishes. The puddings are lush, try the superb Dark Chocolate Mascarpone Cheesecake, you get a huge sticky wedge! Food is served all day and kids are allowed in until 8.30pm.

Horatio's Bar and Victoria Bar
✉ Palace Pier, Brighton
☎ 01273 609361 (general Pier info)

Both bars on the pier have a children's licence and an all day menu, but they aren't the kind of places you go for the food, more just for a laugh! Kids are welcome until 8pm. Horatio's is also a Karaoke Bar - it's so funny to watch sad grown ups who think they can sing embarrass themselves crooning along to Robbie and giving it all the moves like they were on 'Pop Idol'. Just pray the ones you're with don't give it a go.

Infinity Foods
✉ Gardner Street, North Laine, Brighton
☎ 01273 670743

This 'right on' café is the sister place of the Infinity Foods Organic Food shop around the corner. It serves delicious fresh vegetarian / vegan food and is very popular, especially at lunchtimes. You can usually get a seat upstairs, the window seats give a good view of the shoppers outside.

Lucy's Restaurant
✉ King's Road Arches, Brighton
☎ 01273 220222

A really relaxed little place, down by the kid's playground on the seafront generally open when the sun shines but closed when it doesn't! They serve 'posh pub grub' and were voted on of the 'Top 50 Places To Have Breakfast' by 'The Times' newspaper. They have a good kids selection, but there is plenty of stuff on the adult menu too.

Mock Turtle
✉ Pool Valley, Brighton
☎ 01273 327380

This is a very traditional, but cute tea and cakes shop. It looks just like the kind of place your great aunt Ethel would love, but you can't fault her taste 'cos they serve the best cakes in town. Ignore the doilies and the table cloths and get stuck into the scones and the cream slices, then take some home for later.

Moshi Moshi Sushi

✉ Bartholomew Square, Brighton.
☎ 01273 719195

A Japanese experience with a difference. This is a sushi café, where the food is prepared by special chefs in the middle of the room and then placed on a long conveyor belt that travels around the tables. Sushi isn't just raw fish, there are lots of other tasty bits too that are neither raw nor fish, you just pick up and eat what you fancy. You tell the price from the colour of the plate; it is good as you get to see what you are going to eat before it is too late. When you have finished stuffing yourself the waiters count the plates adding up the different prices and then give you your bill. The green horseradish paste called wasabi and the pink pickled ginger are delicious and they are free; the wasabi is also great for unblocking your nose if you have a cold but be careful - it's hot stuff.

Pinocchio

✉ New Road, Brighton
☎ 01273 677676

This is a sister place of Donatello's and so offers the same child friendliness; good food and great value prices. Very handy if you've been swimming at the Prince Regent's Pool or if you've been to the Museum or the Theatre, they are all very close by.

What do you get if you cross a ghost and an Italian restaurant? Spookhetti!!

Terre a Terre

✉ East Street, Brighton
☎ 01273 729051

Now this is a very cool and very lovely vegetarian restaurant. It is the kind of place that makes you feel like giving up meat. They make amazing creations with fancy vegetable crisps coming out at all angles, quite stunning. The puddings are also fantastic - you can hear the Veggies cheer that chocolate is free from meat, the Terre's know how to make it into something to die for. This kind of magnificence makes a special meal, not just your everyday nosh. There is a great kid's menu. Best to book in advance, it is really popular especially at weekends.

Hanging Out - Back to Nature

The Green Bits

Preston Park
✉ Preston Road, Brighton

The biggest and the most popular park in town is Preston Park on London Road, the main road into Brighton. It has lots of facilities; playing fields, tennis courts, bowling greens, a cycle track and a basketball area. It is a great place to go for a picnic or you can try out the café near the tennis courts. Preston Park is where the fantastic free 'Party in the Park' is held every year. You get to see the latest bands - Daniel Beddingfield, Blue, Mis-teeq and the Sugababes have all played before.

> **WHAT IS THE WORST JOB IN THE WORLD?**
>
> One of them has to be dog waste bin emptying. Yes, some poor blokes have to go around and empty all of the little bins full of dog doo doo. Unbelievably they collect over 100 tonnes of dog pooh every year - gross or what?!!

Queens Park
✉ East/West Drive, Brighton

Some people say this is the prettiest park in Brighton. It has a little stream and a lake amongst the beautiful gardens. It tends to be quite quiet, a nice place to escape. There is a tennis court and a bowling green for the oldies and a playground for the youngsters.

Good to go to when town gets too busy in the summer.

Hove Park
✉ Old Shoreham Road, Hove

One of two parks worth a visit in Hove, here you'll find a large open area loved by squirrels, bowls and a cycle track, a playground, miniature railway and, of course, a café.

GET ON DOWN!

You can play this fun game with any number of people - but you'll need at least two. Throw a ball continuously back and forth around the group and whenever any silly fool drops the ball, shout out "Down on one knee". Carry on throwing and if the same person drops it a second time shout "Down on two knees". If the same buffoon drops the ball again you yell "Down on one elbow" and again you scream "Down on two elbows" and finally "Down on your chin" where they have no hope so then they are out. Remember you must stay in the position you're in to catch the ball and throw the ball. Great fun!

St Ann's Well Gardens
✉ Somerhill Road, Hove

This beautiful little park is just up from the main Western Rd in Hove and has been a public park since 1908. It once was the site of an apparently healing spring recommended by the famous Dr Richard Russell, however this shut down in 1935. The best things are the huge playground and the friendly café. There are also tennis courts, a bowls club, a scented garden especially made for the blind and a conservation area with pond.

Stanmer Park
✉ Lewes Road, Falmer

This place is huge! Right up off the A27 next to the University of Sussex it has only been open to the public for 50 years. There is loads of space to just run around, great if you have got a dog. There are also some woods, perfect for playing hide and seek. With lots of little hideaways it is the ideal place for a picnic.

It is especially beautiful in Spring when all of the bluebells come out. The pretty but tiny village of Stanmer is right in the middle of the park; you will find a jolly dairy farm, duck pond and tea shop there as well as the disused 19th century manor, Stanmer House. The park is the location of the Kite Festival every year.

DID YOU KNOW?

When you go into the country there is a Country Code that should be followed. This isn't just some annoying grown up stuff, it's there to protect the animals and you. So do it!!

- Enjoy the countryside and respect its life and work
- Guard against all risk of fire
- Fasten all gates
- Keep your dogs under close control
- Keep to public paths across farmland
- Use gates and stiles to cross fences, hedges and walls
- Leave livestock, crops and machinery alone
- Take your litter home
- Help to keep all water clean
- Protect wildlife, plants and trees
- Take special care on country roads
- Make no unnecessary noise
- Ensure that you jump in all cow pats..(umm that one is made up!)

Bus-Walking

Some clever, environmentally-aware person has come up with an idea called 'take the bus for a walk', not as silly as it sounds. There are a series of walks through the wonderful Downs that you do right from the bus stop. You don't even have to start and finish at the same point. The number

DID YOU KNOW?

The mascot of the number 78 bus is the little wren; a tiny bird with a big voice (like anyone else you know??). There are loads of wrens in Stanmer Park. The no.77 bus has the skylark as its mascot and the number 79 has the yellow hammer. You can often hear the songs of the skylark and the yellowhammer up in the Downs.

HANGING OUT

78 bus from Old Steine and Brighton Station takes you up to Stanmer Park as does the number 25 metro line service from Churchill Square. Number 77 goes up to Devil's Dyke and Number 79 takes you to Ditchling Beacon. If you are travelling with an adult you will go for free (2 free kids with every adult). You can also get a train to Falmer station, Stanmer Park is only a 10 minute walk away.

South Downs

Not only does Brighton & Hove have the spectacular sea; the nearby countryside is also pretty amazing. The South Downs roll behind the city, giving stunning views across Sussex from the highest points.

Devil's Dyke is a great viewpoint; named after its creato. Apparently big D. really didn't like all of the goodie goodies who lived in Sussex and so made the Dyke hoping that it would cause the sea to flood the little villages and drown the churches. However he failed; he got scared off as he mistook an old biddy carrying a candle as the sun rising. Good job too.

On bright days Devil's Dyke is a great place to watch the paragliders or go for a bracing walk, you can also have lunch at the pub.

> **DID YOU KNOW?**
> You can apparently find Fairy Rings on the Sussex Downs, look out for the toadstools. The Sussex word for fairies is 'farisees' or 'pharisees' and they are described as 'little creatures rather bigger than a squirrel and not quite as large as a fox' and they are green in colour and a little mischievous. The most magical place where you might see them, especially at Midnight on Midsummer Eve, is at Chanctonbury Ring on the Downs. Whatever you do, don't laugh at a fairy. They take particular offence at this and might cast a spell on you, so watch out if you do see one!

Sea Life & Land Life

Dolphin Spotting

Did you know that dolphins are seen off the Sussex coast each year? The Sea Watch Foundation regional group has been recording and studying local dolphin sightings since 1991. The species they most frequently see is the bottlenose dolphin which can come quite close to the shore.

Brighton Sea-Life Centre

- ✉ Marine Parade, Brighton
- ☎ 01273 604234
- ⓘ Open Daily 10am-5pm
- £ Costs £5.25 kids (£8.75 Adults, £25 Families)

> **DID YOU KNOW?**
>
> How do you identify Bottlenose Dolphins?
> Bottlenose are 'typical' dolphin shaped and have a small beak. They jump through the waves with a graceful arching motion when they come up to breathe and sometimes leap out of the water. The dorsal fin is sickle-shaped and curves backwards.

Brighton Aquarium is one of the oldest aquariums in the country. In the vibrant Victorian age it was a real treat to see the exotic fish, nowadays it is a bit damp and stinky but it is worth it to see the fishes. As well as the many tanks of exotic fishes there is a touch pool where you can stroke the rays, you can see elegant seahorses and if you're tough enough, go through the shark tunnel. Once you have paid, they stamp your hand so you can go in and out all day. Funnily enough the fish and chips at the café don't quite taste the same afterwards.

> Which sea creature eats its prey two at a time?
> Noah's shark!!!

Drusillas Zoo Park

- ✉ Alfriston, East Sussex.
- ☎ 01323 870234
- ⓘ Open 10am - 5pm summer, 1600 winter
- £ Costs - Kids 3-12 and OAPs £8.49, Over 12's £9.49

Drusillas has been voted the no.1 tourist attraction in the South East and is a great place to spend a day. There is a wide selection of animals all in more natural enclosures including monkeys, crocodile, penguins, bats and snakes as well as more everyday animals in Petworld. Throughout the park you will find exciting hands-on activities like holding and feeling different kinds of animals, helping out at feeding time or you

> Do I need any qualifications to work in the zoo?
> No, you've had plenty of experience with animals already; I've seen your family!!!

can even be a Keeper for the Day. Playland has over an acre of swinging, jumping and climbing obstacles and there is also adventure golf, a discovery centre, a huge bouncy castle and lots more besides. Having your birthday here is the ultimate - you get all sorts of treats including feeding the penguins and having lunch sitting on the birthday throne and it's not too expensive. A must visit place.

Hanging Out - Not To Far Away

Eastbourne
There are lots of things to see and do in elegant Eastbourne, just 21 miles east along the coast from Brighton and Hove. The best place to head for is the Royal Parade and the popular Pier.

Pier Boat trips
☎ 01323 439080
ⓘ Open daily May to September Weekends until Oct and after Easter

You can go on a 45-minute cruise to see Beachy Head (watch out for suicide jumpers - eughhhhh!) and the illuminating lighthouse. Choose between the speedboat '007' or the fast launch 'Jaws' for a thrilling ride on the open sea. You can also see the Seven Sisters, the Crumbles and Birling Gap all spectacular cliffs that are gradually falling into the sea. Boats leave from between the pier and the bandstand every hour between 10am and 4pm.

DID YOU KNOW?
There are in fact eight 'sisters' not seven, from Haven Brow in the west to Went Hill in the east. So there!

Fort Fun
✉ Royal Parade, Eastbourne
☎ 01323 642833

This two-acre fun park features a mega indoor adventure play area as well as an outdoor theme park in the summer. It is for kids up to 12 so you might find some things a bit childish. You can take a ride on the runaway train, rock along the roller coaster, or hop on the bat ride or on the Concorde jet ride. The park also has go-karting and crazy golf.

Sovereign Centre
✉ Royal Parade, Eastbourne
☎ 01323 738822

This great leisure centre has fantastic swimming facilities with 4 different pools. There is the main Gala Pool, a training pool for littlies and a diving pool. The best one is a fun pool that has a surging wave machine, water cannon, bubble jets and a working flume. Cool or what? There is also a ten pin bowling alley.

Trax Indoor Karting Centre
✉ Hampden Park Industrial Estate, Eastbourne
☎ 01323 521133
ⓘ Open daily from 10am-8pm.

This is a proper indoor race track with fast karts, but it is only for those aged over-nine. It is really exciting and quite scary - something different to do for a birthday treat. Michael Schumacher look out!

Treasure Island
✉ Royal Parade, Eastbourne
☎ 01323 411077
ⓘ Open Easter to October, 10am-6pm.

This is another fun park for kids - with lots of activities for all ages up to about 13, so again some things might be a bit young. It has sandpits, paddling pools, a galleon, slides, climbing frames and an indoor play area. It has won awards you know!

Other Places

Lewes Castle and Anne of Cleves House
- High Street, Lewes
- 01273 486290
- Open - Daily (except Mon in Jan & 24-26 Dec)

William the Conqueror told his buddy William de Warenne to get a castle built somewhere around Lewes to defend against the pesky invaders. Shortly after he won the Battle of Hastings the building work started, although they didn't have the best builders in the world as it took nearly 300 years to finish! You get a great view from the top of the castle and you can find out all of the history at the interactive Barbican House Museum next door. Just down the road is Anne of Cleves timber framed house, part of her divorce settlement from her nasty husband, King Henry VIIIth after 6 months of marriage! At least she wasn't beheaded like two of his other wives.

Bluebell Railway
- Sheffield Park Station, Nr Uckfield
- 01825 723777

A vintage steam railway that runs from Sheffield Park to Kingscote travelling on a round trip of 18 miles through delightful unspoilt Sussex Countryside and the longest tunnel on any preserved railway in the country. At Sheffield Park there are the engine sheds to explore and a museum with lots of railway artefacts that were once common place on railways throughout the country, but today are hard to find.

Butlins
- Bognor Regis
- 01243 822445.
- Gates open 9.30am, last admission 6pm

Experience the non-stop entertainment that is Butlins. With Toyland, crazy golf, a go kart circuit, a funfair, the indoor sub-tropical water world, cinema, all weather multi sports court and much, much more. This place is made for kids and families. Whilst it may not be the coolest place around, it is certainly good fun. Loads of people go to Butlins for a weeks holiday, but you can also pop in for a day.

Pooh Corner
- ✉ High Street, Hartfield.
- ☎ 01892 770456
- ⓘ Opening times: 9am to 5pm (Sun 11am- 5pm, BH 1.30- 5pm)
- £ Costs FREE!

Did you have a Pooh Bear or an Eeyore when you were little? If you did then you will love it here. Pooh Corner is the shop where Christopher Robin went shopping with his nanny. It is over 400 years old and has everything you could possibly think of to do with or decorated with the original hunny monster. Nearby is the bridge where CR played pooh sticks, have a go yourself. You can get a free map of the "Enchanted Places" at the shop.

> **DO YOU KNOW?**
> How to find THE bridge where Christopher Robin and Pooh played pooh sticks. Find 'Hartfield Garage', opposite this is a road with a sign restricting cars and other vehicles going down it. Walk down c. ½ mile (800 metres) and you'll find a little wooden bridge over a stream. Although it has been done up in the past, this is the REAL THING. Pretty cool eh?

> **HOW TO PLAY POOH STICKS**
> You need at least 2 players for this:
> Find a nice size stick. Not too big, not too little, just right. Go for one that is quite robust so that it will stay floating if it hits a big leaf or another stick. Always make sure it is bigger than your competitors. Find a bridge to chuck it from, where you get a good view of the river from each side of the bridge. All line up along the bridge - stand at the part of the river where it flows under the bridge the fastest. Drop in your stick in so that it lands flat on the river ready to float fast under the bridge. Race to the other side of the bridge and see your winning stick.

THE ULTIMATE

The Ultimate Day Out

You'll need to arrive early (see the day planner on the next page) if you want to pack everything in, about 10 o'clock would be a good time. You have just got to start at the Palace Pier, the pleasure-packed fortress stretching out into the English Channel. Of course the arcades and rides are great fun; but so is just wandering around watching the waves crash against the strong iron pillars and see the sea gulls dance in the wind.

Pier Highlights

You have got to have a go at the Dolphin Racing; this is really funny, especially playing against your mates or your family. You have to roll a ball until it drops into a point scoring hole. Your dolphin jumps along according to your score; you just have to get your 'Flipper' going faster than everyone else, reaching the finish line first. It is trickier than it sounds but is something that anyone can do; from old grannies to little brothers, worth a go (although the prizes aren't much cop). The horse carousel is also quite fun, all of the horses (and cocks) have names; see if there is one with your name that you can have a go on. The arcades are as good as you can imagine, with all of the latest games and virtual reality simulators. They are expensive; but then this is the ultimate day out. You'll just have to save up or make some money.

Fun on the Seafront

Give yourself an hour on the Pier. Then walk to the left, along the front towards Hove. Pop into the Penny Arcade or the Fishing Museum if either of them takes your fancy. Walk along the bottom by the beach, there are lots of artists displaying their work and sometimes you'll find musicians and singers entertaining the passers-by. On weekends teenagers will be

The Ultimate Day Out

Start	End	What	Why	Cost
1000	1100	Visit the Pier	One of the most visited places in Britain (must be good!) Get a great view of the city from the sea	Approx £5/person If you go in the arcades.
1100	1300	Hang out on Sea front	It's good to relax, take in the sea air You can do a bit of exercise, strolling along the prom or hire some blades You can see the artists - v. cultured	FREE £5 for blades
1300	1400	Fish & Chips on the beach	Cheap and traditional	£4/person
1400	1415	Walk to Museum Gardens	Walk past street entertainers in East Street	FREE
1415	1630	Royal Pavilion or shop in the North Laine	Royal Pavilion is a unique part of Brighton history Very very cultured Shopping lets you get the Brighton vibe	£3.40 kids Have family deals Cost depends on what you buy!
1630	1730	Brighton Museum & Gallery	One of the funkiest museums ever, especially the fashion and design bits. Educational too of course!	FREE
1730	1800	Chill out in Museum Gardens (have a drink in Café)	You'll need a break! Very pretty, an oasis in the city	FREE
1800	2030	Cinema / Bowling / Basketball Your Choice!!	Basketball - the best with top team 'Brighton Bears' Cinema - you just can't beat a good film! Bowling - good family competitive fun	£4 - £7 kids Family deals

THE ULTIMATE

shooting some hoops on the basketball court whilst trendy guys and pretty girls play beach volleyball. Lots just to watch as you wander past.

It's probably time for an ice cream now. Amongst the best are the stripy whippy ice-creams sold right by the children's playground. The mango one is totally delish, especially with a chocolate flake.

If you are feeling energetic then you can hire some equipment from Oddballs at the shop opposite the old West Pier. Whether you fancy kiting, skateboarding, roller skating or roller blading, this is the place to give it a go. If you are after something more sedate then perhaps a gentle stroll or some time relaxing on the beach, skimming pebbles on the sea might be preferable; it is time to chill.

Nosh time!

It will be getting on for lunchtime, the grown ups will be arguing about where to eat. You have many options along the seafront in terms of cafés and sandwich shops. We especially recommend 'Boardwalk' down by the big green bagel, 'Alfresco' the Italian restaurant by the West Pier and 'Rachel's Restaurant' just down from Alfresco. All serve tasty stuff and don't treat you like you are two. Or you could just get haddock and chips from the Chippy and enjoy them on the beach.

The Afternoon

The afternoon will be a little more cultured as you go to the Royal Pavilion and nip into the Brighton Museum and Art Gallery if you have time. You should spend at least two hours in the Royal Pavilion, there is a guided tour at 2.30pm if you fancy it. Afterwards either go to the Brighton

DID YOU KNOW?

The writer William Hazlitt described the Royal Pavilion as 'a collection of stone pumpkins and pepper boxes' whilst another writer William Hone described it as a 'huge teapot all drill'd round with holes' - how would you describe it? Let us know at www.knapsackguides.com.

Museum and Art Gallery or just hang out in the museum gardens.

If this is really not your bag then pop up to the North Laine for a bit of shopping action. Don't miss out on 'Shakeaway' for theeeee most amazing milkshakes in the land.

Last but not least..
Finish the day off in one of 3 ways. The ultimate is to go and see the Brighton Bears play basketball, (weekends) but if they are not playing then either go ten pin bowling or catch a movie in one of the cinemas. You can also snack on a hot dog or a burger at all of these places.

Then it is home to bed after one of the best days ever.

The Ultimate Free Day Out
(well almost free anyway...!)

This is similar to the normal ultimate day as loads of the stuff in Brighton and Hove is free anyway, sometimes just hanging out and wandering around a city can be fun. Again you'll have the early start, arriving about 10 o'clock. The Palace Pier is the place to start, the fun-filled fortress leading you out over the waves. Wander around, take in the view, laugh at grown ups failing miserably at computer games and girls screaming on the scary rides. Good job they got rid of the ghost train! Now watch out for the seagulls, they have got a terrible habit of dropping their doodah right on your head and that can be very messy.

On the Seafront Again!
Allow an hour for the Pier before beginning your stroll past the seasick doughnut along the prom towards Hove. The Fishing Museum is free and relatively interesting, you can always have your photo taken on board one of the little fishing boats. Under the road in the old arches are lots of little shops and art galleries. Further on there is a basketball court where

THE ULTIMATE

The Ultimate Free Day Out

Start	End	What	Why	Cost
1000	1100	Visit the Pier	One of the most visited places in Britain (must be good!). Get a great view of the city from the sea	FREE
1100	1300	Hang out on Sea front	Hang out on Sea front It's good to relax, take in the sea air. You can do a bit of exercise, strolling along the prom or skimming pebbles. Walk up towards Hove. You can see the artists - v. cultured	FREE
1300	1400	Picnic on Hove Lawns	You can bring the stuff you like - all the favourites. Huge grass area to run around on	FREE apart from the picnic
1400	1530	Old Lanes and Museum Gardens	Walk down the Prom and then down Ship Street to the Old Lanes; then down East St to the Museum Gardens. The Old Lanes are steeped in history and are where the smugglers and vagabonds use to hang out - watch out for ghosts	FREE
1530	1630	Brighton Museum & Gallery	Fun and educational at the same time - honestly! Some really cool things to see, including a big section about Brighton in the olden days when your parents were young	FREE
1630	1700	Relax in Museum Gardens	Somewhere pleasant to chat about the day and to plan on what you all want to do next	FREE
1700	1730	Fish & Chips on the beach	Cheap and traditional	£3 to £4/person
1730	1900	Chill on the beach	Sit down by the basketball court and watch the guys net a few baskets or listen to the groovy buskers. If it is hot take a dip whilst the sun goes down	FREE

84

dudes dribble and dunk and a beach volley court where they spike and smash the ball over the net on the sandy pitch. Just so much to see as you meander through the crowds. You might also see skateboarders and BMX bums doing fancy tricks along the ledges and kerbs - some of them are seriously talented. If you have a kite bring this along with you, there are plenty of places to fly it along the front.

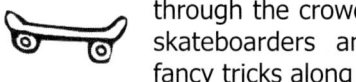

Hove Lawns is a nice picnic spot; there is a mass of space and comfy green grass to lounge around or run about on.

The Afternoon
After lunch wander back towards the Pier, but along the top of the Esplanade this time, good to get a different perspective and you will be able to see the West Pier as it gradually falls apart... Just before you get to the Brighton Centre look out for Ship Street going left on the other side of the road. Nip up here to the Old Lanes where you can potter around and get a feel for how Brighton used to be in the olden days. Sneak into a twitten (alley) and jump out on an unsuspecting grown up! You might get lost in the Lanes but not to worry, just head eastwards and guess what - you will get to East Street. Head along here away from the sea and you will reach the Museum Gardens. You'll probably pass some not bad street entertainers on the way.

Get Cultured!
Next it is into the Brighton Museum and Art Gallery for a bit of local culture. Spend a while in here finding out about what a mad place Brighton & Hove was in the 1950's, 60's and 70's as well the ancient stuff. There are other groovy sections especially if you like art and design. A good place to go to the loo!

Have a relax in the Museum Gardens whilst you decide what to do next. You might be totally totalled and just want to start making your way home, or you

THE ULTIMATE

might be ready for some good old fish and chips down on the beach again. If it is a beautiful sunny day the late afternoon is a great time for a swim, if you are brave enough. Decide what to do and then move on and enjoy whatever you do next.

Eventually you'll be home after a fantastic cheap and cheerful day!!

HANDY STUFF

Listings

Helplines
Childline - free 24hr:
☎ 0800 1111
NSPCC Child Protection Helpline:
☎ 0808 800 5000

Cash Points (handy places to take your parents...!)
Barclays
✉ North Street
Lloyds TSB
✉ West Street
HSBC
✉ Western Road
Nat West
✉ Western Road/ Churchill Square
Bank of Scotland
✉ Dyke Road
Royal Bank of Scotland
✉ North Street
Link Machines
✉ Western Road/ North Street/ Duke Street

Post Offices
✉ 94-101 London Road, Brighton
✉ 51 Ship St, Brighton
✉ 142 Western Rd, Brighton
✉ 120 Church Rd, Hove

Entertainment & Leisure
Bowlplex
☎ 01273 818180
Brighton Centre
☎ 0870 9009100
Brighton Dome/ Corn Exchange/ Pavilion
☎ 01273 709709

HANDY STUFF

Duke of York's Cinema
☎ 01273 602503
Komedia
☎ 01273 647100
Odeon Cinema
☎ 08705 050007
Sealife Centre
☎ 01273 604234
Theatre Royal
☎ 01273 328488
UGC Cinema
☎ 01273 818094

Help!
Emergency Services
☎ **999**
Non emergency Sussex Police
☎ 0845 60 70 999
Lost Property
☎ 01273 665510

Health
Brighton General
☎ 01273 696011
Royal Sussex County (Brighton)
☎ 01273 696955
Royal Alexandra Hospital for sick children
☎ 01273 328145
NHS Direct
☎ 08 45 46 47
Emergency Dentist (yuk!)
☎ 01273 486444

Local Council
Brighton & Hove Council
☎ 01273 290000
Trading Standards Consumer Advice
☎ 01273 292522
Brighton Library
☎ 01273 290800

Hove Library
☏ 01273 290700
Tourist Information
☏ 0906 711 2255
ⓘ (calls cost 50p per minute, UK only)

Museums & Galleries
Booth Museum
☏ 01273 2927777
Brighton Museum & Art Gallery
☏ 01273 290900
Fabrica
☏ 01273 778646
Fishing Museum
☏ 01273 723064
Hove Museum & Art Gallery
☏ 01273 290900
Preston Manor
☏ 01273 290900
Royal Pavilion
☏ 01273 290900

Sport
Brighton & Hove Albion
☏ 0906 8800609
Brighton Bears
☏ 0870 9009100
Brighton Racecourse
☏ 01273 603580
Hove Lagoon
☏ 01273 424842
King Alfred Centre
☏ 01273 290290
Prince Regent Swimming Pool
☏ 01273 685692
Seafront Office (for volleyball court hire)
☏ 01273 292715
Sussex County Cricket Club
☏ 01273 827100

HANDY STUFF

Transport
Local Buses
☎ 01273 886200
London Gatwick Airport
☎ 01293 53 53 53
National Express Coaches
☎ 0870 580 80 80
National Rail Enquires
☎ 08457 48 49 50
Taxis
☎ 01273 414141 / 202020
Tour Bus
☎ 01273 540893
Volks Railway
☎ 01273 292718
Walking Tours
☎ 01273 888596

Web Sites

In Cool Places
www.royalpavilion.brighton.org.uk
www.westpier-trust.demon.co.uk
www.brightonpier.co.uk

With The Rich And Famous
www.chriseubank.net
www.paulmccartney.com
www.gutterandstars.com (Fatboy Slim)
www.bbc.co.uk/drama/faces/nick_berry.shtml
www.dollarsite.co.uk (David Van Day)
www.coogans-run.co.uk (Steve Coogan)
www.emmabuntonofficial.com

Shopping
www.churchillsquare.com
www.choccywoccydoodah.com
www.brighton-marina.co.uk
www.shakeaway.co.uk

Sports
www.brightonbears.com (Basketball)
www.discover-racing.com (Horse Racing)
www.seagulls.co.uk (Football)
www.trap6.com/hove/index.htm (Greyhounds Racing)
www.sussexcountycricket.co.uk
www.kingalfredleisurecentre.co.uk
www.hovelagoon.co.uk

Cultural and Arty Stuff
www.fabrica.org.uk (Weird art Gallery!)
www.virtualmuseum.info
www.brighton-dome.org.uk
www.komedia.co.uk
www.picturehouse-cinemas.co.uk (Duke of York's)
www.brightoncentre.co.uk
www.museums.brighton-hove.gov.uk

Nosh
www.digintheribs.co.uk
www.shakeaway.co.uk
www.moshimoshi.co.uk/brighton.html
www.thedorset.co.uk

Back To Nature
www.vic.org.uk (South Downs Virtual Information Centre)
www.drusillas.co.uk (Zoo)
www.sealife.co.uk

General Info
www.brighton-festival.org.uk
www.brighton-hove.gov.uk
www.brightonwalks.com
www.buses.co.uk
www.gobycoach.com
www.networkrail.com
www.sussexpast.co.uk
www.thisisbrightonandhove.com
www.visitbrighton.com

INDEX

A
Airports 10
Arcades 35-36

B
Basketball 34, 54, 56-57, 62, 71
Beach Football 37
Beach Volleyball 34
Big Green Bagel 36
Blading 50
Blue Flag beach 34
Bluebell Railway 78
BMX 50
Boarding 50
Booth Museum of Natural History 60
Bowlplex 56
Brighton & Hove Albion 56
Brighton & Hove Festival 38
Brighton Bears 57, 83
Brighton Centre 42, 53, 57, 62
Brighton Dome 31, 41, 60
Brighton Museum and Art Gallery 59
Brighton Youth Centre 50
Burning of the clocks parade 17
Buses 37, 73-74, 90
Butlins 78-79

C
Cafés 40, 42, 44, 62-63
Cash Points 87
Celebrities 40-41
Chris Eubank 41, 64
Church Street 43, 54, 60
Churchill Square 43-45, 47, 49, 74
Clothes Shops 44
Coach Travel 12
Countryside 74
Cricket 48, 57

D
Day Planner 9
Devil's Dyke 51, 66, 74

INDEX

Dippers 26
DisabledGo 23
Dolphin Racing 80
Dolphin Spotting 74
Dr Richard Russell 26
Drusillas Zoo 75

E
Eastbourne 76
Eating 62
E-mail 22
Emergencies 19
Emma Bunton 42

F
Fairy Rings 74
Famous People 40-41
Fat Boy Slim 41, 48, 56
Flea Market 42, 44
Food 62
Football 37, 48, 54-57

G
Games Shops 49
Gatwick Airport 10
Gay Pride 17, 38
Geography 28
George IV 26. See also, Prince Regent
George Street 43
Getting Around 14
Getting There 10
Ghosts 29-32
Greyhound Racing 58
Gruesome Bits 29-32

H
Handy Stuff 87
Health 18, 88
Help! 88
Helplines 87
History 25
Horse Racing 58
Hotels 16

INDEX

Hove Lagoon 41, 51, 53
Hove Lawns 50-51
Hove Museum and Art Gallery 59
Hove Park 72

I

International Visitors 20
Internet 22-23, 90

K

Keeping in Touch 21
Kemptown 43-44
King Alfred Leisure Centre 54
Kite Festival 17
Kiting 51
Komedia 61

L

Laine (North) 40, 43-44, 63
Lanes (Old) 25, 29-31, 40, 42, 62
Lewes Castle and Anne of Cleves House 78
Listings 87
Local Buses 14
Local Council 88
London to Brighton bike ride 17

M

Madeira Drive 37, 52
Magazine and Comic Shops 49
Marina 34, 37, 40, 43, 56
Markets 42, 44
Martha Gunn 27, 31-32, 39
Mini Golf 52
Money 9-10, 21
Moulsecoomb Community Sports Centre 55
Murders 29
Museums 59-60, 78, 89

N

Nature 71
Nick Berry 41
North Laine 40, 43-44, 63
Nudist Beach 34, 37

O
Old Lanes 25, 29-31, 40, 42, 62
Old Sussex Words 21
Opening Hours 18

P
Palace Pier 29, 35
Parking 11
Parks 71-75
Party in the Park 17
People 25-26, 28-30
Pheobe Hessel 39
Pitch & Putt 52
Pooh Corner 79
Post Offices 12, 22
Preston Manor 30-31
Preston Park 51, 71
Prince Regent 38-39. See also George IV
Prince Regent Swimming Pool 54
Public Holidays 18

Q
Queen Victoria 28, 38, 59
Queens Park 71

R
Restaurants 34, 43-44, 62-63, 65
Riding 52
Royal Pavilion 26-28, 31, 38, 82
Royalty 26

S
Scout 7 (and throughout book)
Seafront 33-34, 37, 46, 48, 62-63, 66, 69
Sea-Life Centre 75
Shopping 42-43, 90
Sir George Everest 40
Sir Paul McCartney 41
Skateboarding 33-34, 48
South Downs 28, 74
Special Needs 23
Sports Shops 44, 47
St Ann's Well Gardens 72

INDEX

St Luke's Swimming Pool 55
St Nicholas's Graveyard 39
Stanley Deason Leisure Centre 55
Stanmer Park 51, 72-74
Steve Coogan 42
Stoolball 53
Sushi 50, 62, 70
Sussex County Cricket 57
Swimming 51-52, 54-55, 70, 77

T

Taxis 15
Tennis 48, 53-55, 71-72
The Duke of York's Cinema 61
The Lanes 40, 42, 45, 62
The Level 42, 51
The Theatre Royal 61
Toilets! 15
Tourist Information Centre 24
Train / Train Station 10
Travel 10

U

Ultimate Day Out 80
Ultimate Free Day Out 83

V

Vegetarian 71
Volks Railway 37

W

Walking 9-10, 12, 14, 21, 33, 73, 90
Watersports 53
Weather, Weather Statistics 17
Web Sites 90
West Pier 36, 48, 63
What's On 17
White Lady 31
William IV 27
Withdean Stadium / Sports Complex 11, 53, 55-56

Z

Zoë Ball 41
Zoo 75